Modern
Vegetable Gardening

Modern
Vegetable Gardening

Christopher Bird

Lyons & Burford, Publishers

Lyons & Burford
31 West 21 Street
New York, NY 10010.

PRINTED IN THE UNITED STATES OF AMERICA

Design by Lynne Amft Design

10 9 8 7 6 5 4 3 2 1

LIBRARY OF CONGRESS CATALOGING-IN-PUBLICATION DATA

Bird, Christopher.
    Modern vegetable gardening / Christopher Bird.
        p.   cm.
    ISBN 1 – 55821 – 256 – 6
    1. Vegetable gardening.   2. Vegetables.   I. Title.
SB321.B55   1993
635 — dc20   93 – 6128
                                                    CIP

Portions of the information in this book about corn, onions and tomato sauce appeared originally in *National Gardening*. Portions of the information on potatoes and growing tomatoes in hot climates appeared originally in *Organic Gardening*.

FOR ZACK.
MAY THE WORLD
BE HIS GARDEN.

CONTENTS

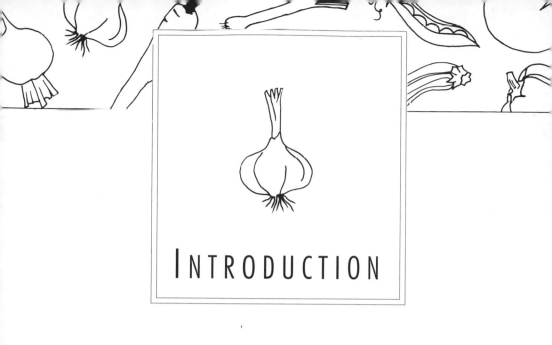

INTRODUCTION

Vegetable gardening came a long way in America during the past 20 years. The most significant innovations have been the organic movement, raised beds, intensive planting, and the whole concept of limited space gardening — all of which are logical developments for the suburban hobbyist, as opposed to our ancestors on the farm. Two hundred years ago we were a nation of farmers. Twenty years ago we were a nation of suburban gardeners, who only *thought* we were still farmers. Today, America is in transition, from backyard gardeners using small-farm methods to backyard gardeners using backyard garden methods.

Regrettably, if garden*ing* came a long way in America these past two decades, most garden*ers* haven't paid attention. Most backyard vegetable growers today still use the same basic techniques our parents or grandparents applied in the 1950's. In fact, the lineage can be traced back, with little evolution (or imagination), thousands of years.

Yet, if we were discovering gardening today for the first time, the rules would be quite different. Why? Because we *live* differently today. Our grandparents lived in the country, and gardened to put extra food on the table, because there wasn't always money to *buy* food. They, in turn, *learned* to garden from ancestors who lived on farms and did *nothing but* grow vegetables. Today, by contrast, most of us live in suburbs, work outside the home, and garden on weekends, for fun and taste.

This book, then, is dedicated to vegetable gardeners who work in (1) their back yards and (2) the 1990's. Unlike gardening books you may have read in the past, this one will not even offer the option of doing things the old way. If you want to garden the way Dad did, buy another book. Better yet, save your money: go to the library. There are plenty of publications still around from the fifties whose counsel will still work. Dirt hasn't changed in the last half of the 20th Century. Neither have shovels. Or bugs.

But just about everything else has. Today there are techniques that can enable you to grow all the vegetables you want, in half the space, with half the work (actually, *less* than half, but if I said a fourth, some of you might not believe me at this point). There are plant varieties that have been bred to grow smaller, resist disease better, and produce bigger and tastier fruit. And, although I'm not an organic purist, there are natural methods for fertilizing and killing insects that are not only better for your health and the environment — they're also easier, cheaper, and more fun.

Most of the techniques presented in this book are ones I discovered myself, through trial and error. But I won't pretend to own the patents. Others have arrived at many of the same conclusions. Gardening personalities like Dick Raymond, Mel Bartholomew, and the late Robert Rodale popularized many of the new techniques in the 1970's and 1980's. I've read just about all the books and subscribed to darn near every gardening magazine I could get my soil-rimmed nails on. What I *haven't* found is any publication that puts all the modern techniques together. Or treats them as the obvious and only way to go for the 1990's and beyond. That's the purpose of this book.

Some of my techniques you *won't* find anywhere else. A few you may even consider bizarre. That's okay. My main goals in gardening are: (1) to grow the tastiest, most eye-appealing vegetables; (2) on the healthiest, most attractive plants; (3) with the least amount of work. All else being equal, I would also like to do it at the lowest cost, and as organically as is reasonable (I'm not going to let caterpillars eat half my lettuce just to prove a point, and I'm not going to introduce wasps into my garden just because they feed on the eggs of other insects).

With the above aims in mind, I feel no loyalty whatsoever to either gardening traditions of the 1950's or cult fads of the 1970's. When it comes to my back yard, I do whatever works best. And so should you.

— Christopher Bird
San Antonio, Texas
November, 1993

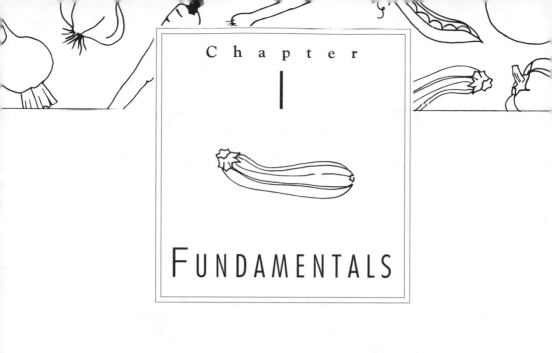

Chapter

I

FUNDAMENTALS

WHO'S IN CHARGE

Though it need hardly be said for experienced gardeners, let's get this out of the way up front for beginners. It's your garden (or will be, if you haven't started). It's your yard. Your dirt. Your seed. Even your bugs. And you must call the shots. In a way, gardening is for the adventurous. Books can only go so far in telling you how to grow things.

To begin with, you will be the one who decides where to locate your garden. Its proportions. Where to purchase fertilizer and soil supplements, while getting the most for your money.

Over the winter, you are the one who must sit down with pen and paper and list what you will grow during the next season. And map out on graph paper what you will plant where. Which requires a determination of how much to grow. And what your family likes to eat, of course. Or what you're tired of growing and want to skip this year. Perhaps there's a new vegetable you'd like to try. Something unusual. Or an "experiment" (I always have at least one going), that may or may not work out. You might want to grow

something mainly for looks, even if you don't particularly enjoy eating it. That's allowed. It's your garden.

Next, you must obtain seed. Since you will be ordering from a seed catalog (this book gives you no other option — you're *not* in charge of *that*), you will want to place as few orders with as few companies as possible, to save on shipping costs. Some companies have better selections, some have cheaper seed. And you must order in time, as well as plant at the right time, to achieve the results you desire. For starting tomato seedlings indoors (this book requires you to start your own), that means sitting down with a calendar and counting backward from transplant time.

You will also want to estimate when a given crop will expire, at least in areas with moderate to long growing seasons, to see if it's worthwhile replacing it with a follow-on crop.

If you've been at this awhile (if you haven't, skip to the next paragraph), what pests afflicted your garden last year? One spring, I grew *GIANT* ornamental cabbage, which cabbage loopers converted to lace. What was worse, the tiny fellows migrated over to the lettuce and spinach, where they ate more than we did. I don't grow ornamental cabbage next to the edible greens anymore, and I grow it in the fall, when caterpillars aren't as much of a problem. Okra attracts aphids in some parts of the country, and if grown next to squash, the aphids can transmit a virus that kills the squash. Obviously, you want to remember your mistakes and learn from them.

Being in charge can be a weighty responsibility. Scared? Don't be. If you space your peppers too closely — or if they grow bigger than you thought they would — you can always remove one (it hurts, I know). If you miss the "window of opportunity" to start your own eggplants indoors, you *can* buy them at a nursery. And if you make a truly bad decision, what the hell. It is only a garden, after all. It's not like you lost the family car in a poker game.

Unlike being in charge of a corporation, being in charge of a garden is something you can do in the privacy of your back yard, or over a cup of coffee and a piece of graph paper. Even timid people can be aggressive when it comes to gardening. And I must say, being in charge is what I like most about raising vegetables. Nothing grows in my garden that I don't want to be there.

WHY GROW YOUR OWN?

Most people think that growing their own vegetables saves money. And it does. But not much. Vegetables are cheap in America, whether we like to admit it or not. If it's cheap for *you* to grow them, it's also cheap for a farmer to grow them *for* you. Factor in government subsidies, plus the fact that farmers and pickers have historically been underpaid for their labors, and it's easy to see why Americans spend a relatively small proportion of their incomes on vegetables. Sure, meat and milk are expensive, because those are expensive commodities to produce. But the typical middle-class family probably saves less than $100 a year by growing its own vegetables.

Some think that home-grown vegetables are more nutritious than those purchased at the supermarket. From a scientific perspective, that's mostly hogwash. Chemically, a squash is a squash and a tomato a tomato, whether grown on your land or Farmer McGregor's. It is true that for some vegetables, fresher produce is slightly more nutritious than not-so-fresh. In other cases, the opposite is true. In a few cases, riper fruit is slightly more nutritious than not ripe, and there *is* a tendency for commercially grown vegetables to be harvested immature, after which they do not always ripen fully. But for the most part, the "more nutritious" argument is just something someone made up because three reasons sound better than two, as in, "Homegrown vegetables are tastier, cheaper, and more nutritious."

Many think that homegrown vegetables are better for your health because they are free of pesticides. Unquestionably, massive use of some insecticides harms our environment, by polluting our air and water, but it has not been shown that eating vegetables grown with the aid of pesticides is bad for your health. And anyway, homegrown vegetables are only pesticide-free if grown without pesticides. If you stick to organics, you must be willing to share a significant portion of your crops with pests, and you must be willing to eat a certain amount of chewed-up, less than appetizing produce. Most of us are not so willing.

Before I talk you out of growing your own vegetables, however (and reading this book), one point is indisputable: the taste and texture of homegrown vegetables are far superior to the qualities of anything you can buy in a grocery store. The biggest reason is freshness. Commercially grown corn is harvested Monday, shipped Tuesday, in your grocery cart Wednesday (if you're lucky), and on your table Thursday (why rush?). *Homegrown* corn can be harvested at 5:30 and on your plate at 6.

Another difference is maturity. Much commercial produce is picked green, before achieving peak flavor, because growers are paid by the pound and a fully ripe pepper or tomato doesn't weigh any more than an almost-ripe one. An early harvest clears space to grow more.

Finally, there is the matter of variety: commercial farmers grow varieties that have been bred to survive machine-harvesting, fit in boxes without wasting space, and ripen in trucks. Varieties bred for backyard vegetable gardens only have to taste good.

If taste is one of the valid reasons to grow your own vegetables, the other is: "for the fun of it." Getting outdoors in the spring sun and fresh air. Working rich, black, crumbly soil with your fingers. Anxiously checking each morning to see if your sweet corn has sprouted or a new squash blossom has opened. Crunching into a sun-warmed bell pepper that is so juicy and sweet you just can't believe the difference between it and the one from the grocery store a week before. Or creating flavorful soups and salads entirely from vegetables *you grew*. If these things don't turn you on, then gardening will be just another chore for you, like mowing the lawn or painting the garage.

Gardening *is* a certain amount of work. But not much (and entirely pleasurable at that), if you follow the recommendations in this book. Here's the first such recommendation: keep it small. You don't need a quarter-acre garden in order to have a fresh vegetable to eat each night and even give some away. One hundred square feet or less may do it.

Most gardeners grow too much of some things — sometimes *way* too much. Zucchini is the classic example. Grow more than one plant and you'll have the stuff coming out your ears. You'll bake it, stuff it, sauté it, boil it, freeze it, and give it away. You'll grind it up and ingeniously incorporate it into recipes that don't call for it and to which it adds nothing in flavor or texture, but in the end there are only so many ways to "hide" it in your cuisine

—zucchini bread, zucchini cake, beef stew with zucchini....We all know the ritual.

Another good example is tomatoes. Most people think they have to grow three to six plants (perhaps because that's how many come in a tray at the nursery), but the truth is, one healthy plant will provide the average family a nice fresh tomato several times a week. Okay, maybe you do want to cook homemade spaghetti sauce. So grow two plants. The point is, why grow more of anything than you can use?

Of course, you can always "put up" what you can't eat fresh. But if what you're after is fresh taste, why do a lot of canning and freezing? That *is* work. Canning materials cost money. So does freezer space. And when you're done, you'll have succeeded (*if* you're successful) in replicating Del Monte canned beans or Birdseye frozen corn.

Limited space gardening is not only less wasteful than traditional methods, it's easier, too. Every gardener wants good dirt. But it takes hundreds of hours of hard labor and years of patience to get good dirt when you begin by staking out a 25 × 25 foot patch of unimproved ground. It's easy when you start small. It's also easy to *keep* a small garden — easy to keep it weeded, fertilized, watered, pest-free, and attractive.

In the final analysis, it's much more satisfying to garden on a small scale and do it to perfection than do it up big time but make a mess of it. And if small is enough, why do more?

GARDENING BASICS

Though this book will tell you the best ways to plant and grow vegetables in your back yard in the 1990's and beyond, this is the only section *not* designed to support that end. The purpose of this section, rather, is to introduce beginning gardeners to the most rudimentary aspects of vegetable gardening as it has traditionally been practiced, so that we will have a common starting point. What follows, then, is a sort of VEGETABLE GARDENING 1950.

When I first decided some years ago (later than the 50's) that I would like to try growing my own vegetables, I was almost as ignorant about the subject as someone who had just arrived from another planet. I knew generally that seeds went in the ground and plants needed water. I had some vague notion that plants also needed fertilizer or manure or something. I had heard such terminology as spade, cultivate, and "work the soil," but didn't really know what it meant. I wasn't sure what a hoe was for or under what circumstances one might apply a shovel to the garden. To someone raised on a farm, knowledge such as the above must seem so basic as to be obvious. But if you grew up in a city or, like me, a suburb, and in a non-gardening family, where do you begin?

I realize now that there are books on the subject. But frankly, most of the books I own today on gardening would have been beyond my grasp at that stage. So I started asking friends questions.

"How deep in the garden should I plant my tomato seeds?"

They would give me puzzled looks. "You don't plant seeds (dummy), you plant transplants."

"Where do I *get* transplants?"

"Why, the nursery, of course."

"How big does a tomato plant get?"

"That depends on what type it is, and whether you stake it or cage it."

"Stake? Cage?"

"Well, sure. You're going to give it some support, aren't you?"

"Do other plants come as transplants besides tomatoes? Corn, maybe?"

(Laughter) "Corn comes in seeds. Everything comes in seeds. Except the things that don't."

I would try to shift the conversation.

"How do I know where to *put* my garden?"

"Just pick a spot in the back yard."

"And just stick the seeds and transplants right through the grass?"

(More laughter) "Well, I assume you're going to dig up the grass."

"Of course I'm going to dig up the grass."

Sound familiar? Okay, let's start with some basics.

Most vegetables, like tomatoes, corn, cucumbers, peppers, beans, and squash, do best in warm weather — say, 80–90 degrees Fahrenheit during the daytime. They do poorly in cool weather and usually die if temperatures dip below freezing. Other plants, such as lettuce, spinach, cabbage, cauliflower, broccoli, peas, and onions, like cool weather, and thrive in daytime temperatures of 50–60. Most in this group will survive some frost. And a very few plants, notably okra and sweet potatoes, do best in hot weather, with temperatures in the nineties or even over 100. What all this means, of course, is that some plants will do better in some climates than others. It also means you should plant different things at different times of the year.

Most vegetable plants like full sun. Gardens don't do well in areas that get shaded by trees or fences for much of the day. And plant heights are import-ant — you don't want to plant tall-growing plants where they will shade out smaller plants. Although the sun's position varies throughout the day, on av-erage it shines in at a slight angle from the south (even at noon, when we normally think of it as being directly overhead). So it is best to plant tall plants in the northern part of the garden, with smaller plants to the south.

Virtually any plant can be grown from seed, and most usually are. How-ever, some plants take so long to mature and produce fruit that it is custom-ary to extend the growing season by starting them indoors in small pots a month or two in advance of putting them out in the garden. Examples are tomatoes, eggplants, and peppers, which take four to five months from seed to produce their *first* mature fruit, and longer than that to produce a *signifi-cant quantity* of fruit. You can buy seed and start your own plants indoors, or, at the proper transplanting time, you can go to a nursery and buy small plants, which someone *else* started from seed. Most gardeners do the latter.

Other plants, including corn, peas, beans, okra, spinach, carrots, and radishes, are normally direct-seeded into the garden. This is the best approach for obtaining healthy plants when there is no need to start from transplants. It is also, of course, the simplest method. And for crops like carrots, where each plant produces only one "fruit," it would be ridiculous to start 100 plants indoors, not to mention the fact that root crops don't transplant well anyway.

Some plants can be started either way. This category includes squash, lettuce, onions, cabbage, and melons. In cool climates, with short growing seasons, transplants are preferred.

Another reason to start seedlings indoors is that many are quite delicate. A windblown twig or large raindrop can kill a cabbage seedling. Forgetting to water on a hot, dry day can kill a baby tomato that was direct-seeded in the garden. A stray cat scampering through your garden is not likely to kill hardy seedlings like corn or squash, but a careless pawprint can sure mash the heck out of a three-day-old pepper.

A few vegetable plants are difficult to start from seed. When planting potatoes, for instance, you normally plant a piece of a potato, with an "eye," which will send up a shoot. When planting sweet potatoes, you plant a cutting. And a few rarely grown plants, like horseradish, you start front a piece of root.

Most plants produce blossoms, which develop into fruit. Some plants, like squash, have both male and female blossoms, in which case only the female flower sets fruit but a male flower must be open simultaneously for pollination. That's why we have bees. Some plants, like tomatoes and peppers, have bisexual blossoms (horticulturists call them "complete" blossoms), which are essentially self-pollinating, only you still need a bee (or wind) to get in there and stir things up.

Spacing is an important consideration, to provide adequate room for both top and root growth, as well as adequate sunlight. Traditionally, gardens have been planted in rows, allowing space for walk paths. Corn seed has

Female squash blossom, with immature, unpollinated fruit attached.

traditionally been planted every two inches within a row, then thinned to one-foot spacing after emergence, with 36 inches between rows. Squash and tomato plants have customarily been spaced two to three feet apart within rows, with twice that much space between rows. (Don't remember what you just read — these are not the spacings you and I will be using!) Pepper plants require somewhat less space. Onions, carrots, spinach, lettuce, peas, and beans are planted still closer together.

Plant heights depend on the particular variety (some types of tomato grow bigger than others), spacing, your climate, and how well you care for your garden. However, tall plants, say, 5–7 feet, generally include corn, okra, peas, and pole beans. Medium plants, around 2–4 feet tall, include tomatoes, peppers, eggplant, and squash. Low-growing plants include radishes, turnips, spinach, lettuce, and cabbage. Vining plants, like melons and pumpkins, send out runners over the ground (rapidly!).

14

Some plants require support if they are not to sprawl all over your garden. Tomatoes have traditionally been "staked"—pruned to one stalk and tied to a six-foot stick hammered into the ground. Peppers and eggplants also frequently require support. Pole beans and peas are grown on trellises, stakes, cyclone fences, or rows of string.

How much to plant is always a difficult question for new gardeners. We once had a neighbor who planted 100 tomato plants (they filled his back yard), because he wanted to harvest 100 tomatoes! He didn't know that a typical tomato plant may produce 25 tomatoes! Most plants, including tomatoes, squash, okra, peppers, eggplants, peas, and beans, produce a few fruit at a time, throughout the season. Some plants, like spinach, lettuce, and cabbage, don't actually produce fruit—you eat the leaves—but can be harvested continually. Other vegetables, such as radishes, carrots, turnips, and onions, do indeed produce but one fruit or root per plant. A single corn plant normally produces two ears of corn, about a week apart. A traditional family garden, then, might include three tomato plants, three pepper plants, one eggplant, 20 corn plants, and three squash plants, during the main summer growing season. Spring and fall gardens might contain a four-foot row each of radishes, carrots, onions, turnips, cabbage, and lettuce.

All gardens attract bugs, insects, and caterpillars. Not knowing that someone planted the garden, for consumption by the humans who live in the nearby house, these pests think they've discovered a natural, bountiful supply of fresh food. They not only tend to hang around the garden, but tell their friends about it and flourish and multiply. Many gardeners spray insecticide every week or two. Hard-line organic gardeners try to pick the beasts off by hand, or spray them off with water hose and nozzle, and as a last resort spray insecticidal soap or similar organic (but seldom effective) concoctions. You can, of course, just accept the fact that bugs are going to destroy a certain portion of your crop; that's what farmers did 100 years ago. Most gardeners probably fall somewhere in between, *preferring* organic methods but spraying insecticide on a limited basis when needed.

All plants do best in loose, crumbly dirt, which makes it easy for roots to grow. The best soil contains lots of organic matter, or "humus," which helps retain moisture, keeps the soil loose (or "friable"), and also provides some nutrients. Before you establish your garden, most of the soil in your yard will probably be hard-packed and contain some undesirable things like clay or rock. The traditional solution is to take a shovel, remove any grass, and then break up the soil down to a depth of at least 8–12 inches (this is the function a plow performs on farms). In the process, you remove any large rocks, clay, or buried builder's debris. As you break up the dirt (you probably will have to use your hands), you also work in some organic matter, such as peat moss, bark mulch, leaves, or "compost" (more on composting later).

All plants need water, of course. In most parts of the country, an inch of rain a week is considered adequate, and if you're fortunate enough to live in a climate where rain is plentiful, you may seldom need to turn on the sprinkler. For seeds to sprout, and for young plants with shallow root systems to survive, it's advisable to moisten the soil every day.

What many *new* gardeners *don't* understand is that plants also need good *drainage*. Soil with lots of clay and rock, or even good soil that is *surrounded* by such materials, does not drain well. When plants continually stand in wet, mucky soil, they rot — or, at best, fail to grow — since healthy roots require air as well as water.

Plants also need nutrients. Rarely does soil in its natural state contain enough of the nutrients garden plants need to really do well. And even if you were lucky enough to have the nutrients, continual gardening in the same plot of land would eventually deplete them. The three main nutrients are nitrogen, phosphorous, and potassium. Nitrogen makes for green, leafy growth, while phosphorous and potassium make for healthy plants, and good root and fruit production. Too *much* nitrogen can make for all leaves and no fruit. Most gardeners sprinkle commercial fertilizer on their garden or work it into the top few inches of soil. A bag of "5–10–5" fertilizer is 5% nitrogen, 10% phosphorous, and 5% potassium — this is traditionally the formula used for vegetable gardening. It is also possible to provide necessary nutrients "organically." For example, manure is very high in nitrogen. But this is tricky business, best left for experienced gardeners or organic purists, and, in any case, it is not what most gardeners traditionally do.

THE ELEMENTS

There are four fundamental factors that must be right for successful vegetable gardening: soil, sun, heat, and water. Sounds basic, doesn't it? That's the problem. It's so obvious that even veteran gardeners sometimes don't pay enough attention to these factors.

SOIL

If you love to garden, you also love the look and feel of rich, black, crumbly soil. One affinity doesn't come without the other. But I can almost guarantee that you will not start out with dirt like that in your back yard. Soil consists of four main components: sand, clay, silt, and humus. Those components come together naturally in different proportions in different parts of the country.

Areas of the country that are within 100 or 200 miles of the coast tend to have soil that is predominantly sand. So do most deserts. The *good* things about sand in your garden are that it keeps the soil loose and workable, it's easy for roots to grow in, and it drains well. The latter property is also the *bad* thing: it doesn't *retain* water well. Sandy soil needs to be watered frequently. Some vegetables do best in soil with a high sand content — the best examples are spinach, and root crops such as carrots, potatoes, and onions. Most vegetables could theoretically be grown in *pure* sand, if given sufficient water and fertilizer.

Clay is the densest of soil components. It's gummy and sticky when wet, and hard as a brick when dry (after all, it's been made into pottery for thousands of years). Clay can be white, red, brown, or variegated (such as Alaska "native clay," which makes beautiful ceramics). A *little* clay in your garden soil is good, but *too much* hinders root growth. It hurts in two ways: (1) it's too dense for roots to grow through, and (2) it's too prone to waterlogging.

Humus is spongy, decaying organic matter, and is by far the most important component of garden soil. It retains moisture well, provides an easy growing medium for plant roots, and also provides some nutrients. Naturally occurring humus comes mainly from rotting leaves, branches, and dead roots. Humus co-produced by man may come from grass clippings, straw, kitchen waste, or "compost." Compost is dark, crumbly matter that results from piling up a variety of organic material, with the deliberate intent of letting it decay and then tilling it into your soil. There are many other organic substances you can dig into your soil to add humus, the most widely available being bark mulch and peat moss.

Silt consists of fine particles of powdered rock, found naturally on river and lake bottoms. It is sometimes passed off as "topsoil" by landscaping companies. And it's not *bad* for gardening. Neither is it particularly *good*. It's just there.

Technically, topsoil is the relatively fertile top layer of substance covering earth's land masses (as opposed to the poorer substrata), which is most suitable for plants to grow in. Beyond that, however, the word topsoil means different things to different people. In nature, the black, acidic dirt that results from fallen, decaying leaves in a forest is the best example of topsoil. In some parts of the world, volcanic ash constitutes a significant proportion of the topsoil. As noted earlier, when you order a truckload of topsoil, or buy a bag at the nursery, you may actually get silt. Or compost in a very advanced stage of decay. Or various combinations of sand, silt, and organic matter.

The best soil for gardening in general is mixture of all of the above, with the emphasis on humus and sand, in that order, and relatively little clay. You can create what is commonly called "garden loam" by combining one part sand with two parts topsoil. By adding liberal amounts of organic matter, an ideal growing medium results.

SUN

After soil, sun is probably the next most important element for successful gardening. As we observed earlier, most vegetable plants do best in full sun. The sun rises in the east, sets in the west, and shines in from a slightly southerly direction throughout the day. This means that you don't want to plant your garden along the northern wall of your house, where it would be in shade most of the day, but you could plant along a southern wall. It also means that *within* your garden, you don't want to plant corn directly to the south of tomatoes.

Midday sun is much stronger than morning or afternoon sun. The reason for this is that early and late in the day, when the sun is low in the sky and shines in at an extreme angle, the light must pass through more atmosphere, which filters out much of the ultraviolet radiation. For my own calculations, although I have no scientific evidence to base it on, I generally estimate that the sunlight between 10:30 AM and 1:30 PM Standard Time (11:30–2:30 Daylight Savings Time) is about twice as strong as the sun from 9 to 10:30 or 1:30 to 3, which in turn is twice as strong as the 7:30–9 or 3–4:30 sun. The contribution of sunlight to plant growth before 7:30 AM or after 4:30 PM is negligible. So about 85–90% of a plant's useable sunlight comes between 9 AM and 3 PM (10 AM–4 PM DST). This means that if your garden is in an area that gets early morning or late afternoon shade, it doesn't make much difference.

If you have a heavily wooded lot, you'll be wasting your time to try to have a vegetable garden unless you're prepared to do some clearing (and stump and root removal) or else have an "open" area somewhere, albeit a less-than-desirable garden location (I once had a garden in our front yard, for just that reason). If you have a wooded lot and do decide to garden in an open area, you would be well advised to observe the sun patterns over the course of an entire growing season before rolling up your sleeves. After June 21, the sun gets lower in the sky, and an area that is mostly sunny in June could be mostly shady by August!

In some hotter parts of the country, plants actually benefit from partial shade during the heat of summer. Tomatoes, for example, seldom set fruit when the temperature is much above 90. And although some other plants will both survive and produce fruit in 100-degree heat, their seeds will not germinate. Southern gardeners often use plastic mesh to provide filtered shade.

At the other extreme, neither tomatoes nor peppers will set fruit if night-time temperatures drop much below 50. Northern gardeners frequently use cold frames to extend the growing season. More on cold- and hot-climate gardening in later chapters, but for now, suffice it to say that heat and sun are inseparable factors.

Pay close attention to recommended planting dates. These vary by region and, of course, the species of plant. It's a waste of effort (and garden space) to try to grow warm weather crops during the cooler times of year, and vice versa. Worse, you may be missing out on growing something else that *would* be doing well. To get the most from your garden, you want to take full advantage of the "window of opportunity" for each plant. This is especially true in extreme climates.

Many vegetable plants take their cues from changing day lengths and heat patterns over the course of the growing season. Spinach "goes to seed" as the days get longer and warmer in spring. Onions grown in the North, called "long day onions," direct their energy to green top growth as days lengthen in spring, then form bulbs as the days shorten after June 21. In the South, the opposite is true: "short day" onions are planted in the fall, don't start bulbing until January, and are harvested in late spring.

WATER

Finally, as has already been stated, all plants need water. Soil should be kept moist, not wet, and just slightly moist, at that. When the top two inches of dirt are dry, it's time to water. If you've prepared your soil properly, applying a sprinkler for an hour twice a week in summer should be about right in most parts of the country, if you don't get rain. (You may have to water a little more or less frequently in extreme climates.) If you have time to kill, or simply enjoy the tranquilizing effect, hand-spraying with a nozzle set on fine mist is equally effective — each area of the garden should be misted for about 10 continuous minutes, in that case. You can try hand-watering without a nozzle, but totally dry soil tends not to absorb water well; it's best to dampen it slowly; otherwise, water just runs right through. However you water, do it early in the day, to minimize evaporation by the sun (evening watering minimizes evaporation loss even more, but leaves your garden wet all night, which encourages fungus).

I don't recommend underground drip systems. They're a lot of trouble to install, the connections tend to come apart (you won't know it until you're done watering and find your garden still dry, except for one area, which is soaked), and they get in the way when you dig and work the soil. They normally come with about 20 feet of small-gauge hose to get from the spigot to your garden, which is fine if your garden is less than 20 feet from the house. Otherwise, you'll have to run a garden hose from the faucet to the drip system, and the pressure backup may eventually cause the garden hose to leak or split (if you bury the *garden* hose too, like I once did, you may never realize it has split). Nor do drip systems water as evenly as the manufacturers would have you believe. Unless you space the hoses more closely than the instructions recommend, the soil directly under each hose receives more moisture than the soil to the sides. And if the water is "hard" in your part of the country, it will eventually clog up the pores in a drip system.

MULCH

Covering exposed soil surfaces with a layer of mulch helps to cool the soil and conserve moisture during summer. That's true everywhere in the country, but in hot or dry regions it is *essential*. Grass clippings are the cheapest and most readily available source of mulch for most of us. And they retain moisture better than anything else. Allow clippings to dry some first, then apply an even, one-inch layer over the entire soil surface. It's best not to water right away, since you want the clippings to continue to dry, so apply the mulch when you don't plan to water for 24 hours (but not immediately *after* watering, as the soil surface should not be damp). Mulch shrinks as it decays, and grass clippings shrink faster than coarser mulches, so re-mulch monthly, keeping the depth at about one inch. If you dump much more than an inch or two of fresh, green clippings all at once, the bottom of the layer may turn to slime. Dry, straw-like clippings are best. The time to start mulching is when hot weather sets in.

You can mulch with other things besides grass clippings. Bark mulch looks better. Around squash, cucumbers, and melons, it is also more effective, since slugs love to snack on those fruits at night and find grass clippings a very comfortable environment to laze around under during daytime. (Slugs are like snails without shells and probably find bark mulch too rough on their bodies.) Bark mulch is also a more enduring soil improvement than grass clippings, when at the end of the growing season (or when you pull an expired member of your garden and plant something new), the old mulch gets dug back into the soil. On the other hand, you have to pay for bark mulch, and drive up to the store to get it. I believe in doing things cheaply and easily, all else being equal. And like most gardening fanatics, I don't like to let stuff like grass clippings go to waste. So I use grass clippings on most of my garden, reserving some bark mulch for the above vegetables and for plantings in which aesthetics are important to me. Pick a fine bark mulch, since it holds moisture better and, later, breaks down into the soil faster than coarser bark mulch.

Some gardening books recommend other mulches — leaves, peanut shells, rice hulls. Forget it. The authors are just trying to fill space in their books. Leaves mat down. *Shredded* leaves blow away. I guess if you live near a Planter's factory or Uncle Ben's, you can probably get a free supply of the other stuff. But don't pay for it at a nursery. There are too many cheaper (or free) sources.

So there you have it. The elements, as nature chose to bless (or deny) your yard. Most plants can accept some variance in soil, sun, heat, and water conditions. However, it is often hard to convince beginning gardeners that each element is important. Do it right, and your garden will thrive. Neglect these factors, and your garden will fail. It's really true.

RAISED, INTENSIVE BEDS: THE ONLY WAY TO GO

It's probably because I grew up in the suburbs, rather than on a farm like my parents (and also because I'm a natural nonconformist), that the old methods of gardening never made any sense to me. Why should you break your back

A raised, intensive bed, full of summer vegetables.

digging and clod-busting a strip of ground that's only going to be used to walk on? If tomato plants need 18–36 inches between them *within* a row, why do they need 36–60 inches *between* rows? And, at the risk of sounding like an aging yuppie, why should you sweat it out year after year, trying to gradually turn rocks, clay, and builder's debris into dirt, when you can nail together some boards and instantly fill a raised bed with the richest soil imaginable?

Although raised beds first became popular in this country during the seventies, they have been used in northern Europe for centuries. Establishing one can be as simple as mounding dirt up. Alternatively, you can build a frame out of railroad ties, landscape timbers, or (my personal preference) plain old, two-inch thick lumber, and fill it with dirt. Framing, which is similar to what I've seen in Europe, is clearly preferable, because it keeps the soil from eroding away. The mounded dirt approach is an idea, typical of the current "transitional" U.S. gardening era, that simply hasn't been thought all the way through to its logical conclusion.

There are three main advantages to gardening "above ground" versus "below." First, raised beds drain well, which is important if you live in an area that receives too much rain at certain times of year — especially if the soil nature provided you is high in clay content and tends to retain water. Second, raised beds provide warmer soil, since the sides of the bed receive sun along with the upper surface. This is of interest chiefly to those who live in cool climates and want to extend the growing season. However, it is also beneficial to those in extremely *hot* climates, where gardening tends to be concentrated into brief spring and fall seasons. The third advantage is that you can control what goes in a raised bed. Rather than "improving what you've got," which is what gardeners have traditionally done, you start from scratch. This is the most valuable benefit in general, but it is critical in regions with little or no topsoil.

A natural ally of raised beds is "intensive gardening," which is just a fancy term for grouping plants close together and eliminating walk paths. Raised beds make it easier to create deep "good soil." The deeper your improved soil goes, the deeper roots can grow, and the closer you can space plants (within reason). Intensive gardening thus allows you to grow more in less space. Which means less area to maintain. It also means that the soil you *do* maintain is easier to work, because it never gets walked on and compacted. Intensive gardening has been practiced in the Far East, out of necessity, for even longer than raised beds have been used in Europe.

Our parents gardened in rows. It's a lot of work to dig the soil in a 20 X 20 foot garden only to waste 50% of it on walk paths, but how else could you get in to weed, prune, stake, spray, and harvest without trampling the very plants you were trying to nurture? This way of thinking was a carryover from our farm heritage: on farms, space is plentiful and the difficulty of digging the soil not a consideration (because you use a plow). It was also thought 25 years ago that extra root growth occurred between rows; we know today that's not true, because constant trampling compacts the dirt beneath the walkways too much.

Paths do allow extra light in, but if you site your plants carefully and don't let tall plants shade out smaller ones, all plants in an intensive garden will receive ample sun. Some rules of green thumb for intensive gardening: Space plants in all directions at the distance traditionally recommended for *within* rows; ignore the recommended spacing *between* rows; for different types of plants, split the difference. Locate tall plants to the north and small plants to the south, with in-between ones in between.

Without paths, however, you must keep your growing beds narrow, so that you can reach into every part of the garden. Four feet width is about right for most people, since the average person can comfortably reach two feet. Don't be tempted to go much wider. You may think you have a three-foot reach, but it's difficult to squat and do manipulative tasks much beyond two feet without losing your balance and bringing your hand crashing down on the carrots. Your beds can be as long as you like — six feet, 10 feet...it's your choice.

4 × 4 foot squares are especially convenient. For one thing, they lend themselves to plant groupings. You can put four tomato plants in one 4 × 4 bed, or four squash plants, or nine okra plants, or 16 corn plants. A bed this size is about right to grow the right amount of one type of vegetable for one family. Of course, you're not limited to that. You can always put two tomatoes and three peppers, say, in one bed.

4 × 4 beds also allow more sun in than longer beds. And they simplify the problem of tall plants casting unwanted shade on small plants, because you have fewer different types (and heights, therefore) of vegetable in each bed. In hot climates, 4 × 4 beds also simplify shading the plants you *want* to shade; you can plant tomatoes, for example, where they will receive afternoon shade from your okra. Regardless of your climate, shade can be used to extend the lives of light- and heat-sensitive crops like spinach and peas.

Finally, 4 × 4 foot beds make crop rotation more effective, by segregating soil from different crops. Crop rotation is something I like to do, other

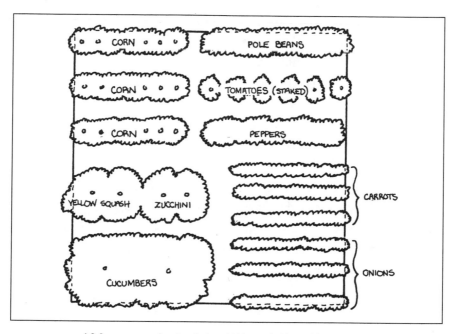

400 square feet of traditional ''row'' garden.

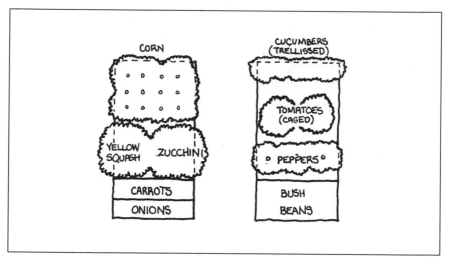

64 square feet of intensive garden.

considerations being equal, and it is something you *should* do if the layout of your garden facilitates it. (More on crop rotation later in the book.)

On the minus side, numerous small beds are harder to mow and edge around than a few long beds. But all in all, I believe 4 × 4 foot beds offer ideal versatility. Having said all that, I must confess that, as I write this, most of my current beds are 4 × 6. The layout of my yard just didn't lend itself to 4 × 4 squares. You work with what you've got.

Credit Mel Bartholomew, in his now-classic *Square Foot Gardening*, with popularizing intensive planting in the U.S., although a number of people thought of the idea about the same time. Dick Raymond, in *Joy of Gardening*, advocated "wide row" planting (another "transitional" idea), figuring that by planting two narrow rows of vegetables contiguously you could eliminate one walk path.

Individually, neither raised beds nor intensive planting is new. Yet, each time they are discussed, it's as if they were. Moreover, they are presented as options — alternatives to the "real" methods — on which gardeners still must be sold. It's particularly surprising how few gardeners apply both concepts simultaneously as their main way to grow vegetables. As someone who learned to garden in the seventies and eighties, I say it's time to embrace raised, intensive beds as the standard way of prosecuting our craft. This much is certain: If you are a beginning backyard vegetable gardener in the 1990's, there is no point in learning how to be a farmer in the 1950's.

Chapter

2

GETTING STARTED

ESTABLISHING RAISED BEDS

Your first step is to decide how many and what size beds you want. If in doubt, a good start would be four 4 × 4 foot beds. 64 square feet of intensive, raised garden will put a surprising amount of fresh vegetables on the table if well tended (and it's so easy to tend a small garden well!). Especially if what you're after is simply a fresh vegetable to eat every night, without a lot of canning, freezing, and pickling.

Buy some lumber. Pressure-treated lumber is somewhat more expensive, but it resists rotting and is worth it in my opinion. Plain old untreated pine also works, and should last from three to eight years, depending on your climate and how much you use your garden. Continual moisture hastens rotting action, as does a warm climate in which microorganisms are active year-round.

2 × 6 inch boards are most commonly used. I use 2 × 12's. Six inches of good dirt is not deep enough to grow some things, like tomatoes, corn,

squash, or okra. It will grow peppers and small plants like spinach, lettuce, and radishes. To have a successful garden that will grow anything, six-inch, deep beds require another six inches of fairly good dirt down below your raised beds. In my yard, you'd literally have to blast rock to arrange that. Whatever depth you choose, it's still better to work the soil underneath if you can.

Saw and nail the boards into frames. Don't try to build a piece of furniture. The kind of lumber you'll be using is bound to have warps and broken edges here and there. Try to put any unsightly spots where they won't show, but don't expect the boards to fit perfectly. Obviously, use large nails. A 2 × 12 frame will stay together better if you use four nails per joint and drive them in at opposing angles. When your "sandboxes" are complete, position them where you want them on your lawn. Allow at least two feet—three is better— between boxes. If possible, try to orient the frames with the sides north-south and east-west, as this will facilitate positioning most plants for optimum sunlight. Pick your spots well, because once the boxes are filled with dirt, they're not going anywhere. (There is no need to anchor them.)

If you intend to work the soil beneath your raised beds (this is called "double-digging"), once you have the boxes positioned, outline the insides of the frames on the lawn with a can of spray paint. Then move the boxes aside and start digging. First remove the top two or three inches of sod and turn it upside down in the sun somewhere to dry. The object now is to dig a flat-bottomed, rectangular pit in the shape of each frame. Separate the stuff you remove (by hand, if necessary) into two piles—relatively good soil, which you want to return to the pit (pile it on a plastic sheet so that you don't lose any); and poor soil, rock, clay, and buried builder's debris, which you want to cart away. The deeper you dig, the better your garden will be, but a total "good soil" depth of 12 inches, counting your raised bed plus whatever (if anything) you improve underneath, is adequate. 18 inches would be outstanding.

A new 4 × 4 foot raised bed being constructed out of 2 × 12 inch lumber.

When you've dug as far as you intend to, line the bottom of each pit with the sod you removed, upside down and broken into pieces. Sod normally consists of good topsoil and good organic matter and will be a healthy addition to your garden. Putting it in the bottom of the pit insures it won't grow up into your raised bed. Now it's time to start refilling the pit with the good dirt you took out, breaking up clods with your shovel or hands as you go. Add some humus. And some topsoil if your property is sandy, or sand if your soil is dense and black and sticky. Otherwise, the dirt will eventually just return to its original state (or else, don't double-dig to begin with).

When you final-position your wooden frames, try to make them level, even if your yard is not. Use a carpenter's level if you have one, or at least a glass of water. (Remember that what counts is the levelness of the soil surface, not the top edge of any one board.) If you double-dug, you may want to push one portion of the frame down into the dirt. Otherwise, place rocks or clay under the frames here and there to make the boxes level. If this leaves spaces at the bottom, plug them, so that your soil won't wash away out the bottom. Rolled-up newspapers tied with string are good for wedging into the open spots. They're organic and will decompose eventually.

If you don't want to double-dig (or if your soil won't permit it), consider using a "foundation" frame, made out of 2 × 4's, under a 2 × 12 "main frame." Since 2 × 4's are really 1 1/2 × 3 1/2, and 2 × 12's are really 1 1/2 × 11, this will provide a total "good soil" depth of at least 14 inches, even if your boxes are not absolutely full to the top. (Plus, some root growth can still occur in the natural soil beneath your raised beds, even if it's compacted.) Don't expect the 2 × 4 foundation frame to line up perfectly with the 2 × 12 frame. Apply a few small nails at strategic spots, to keep the 2 × 12 frame from sliding around on the 2 × 4 frame while you're positioning your bed and filling it with dirt.

An extra deep bed, comprising a 2 × 12 ''main'' frame atop a 2 × 4 ''foundation'' frame.

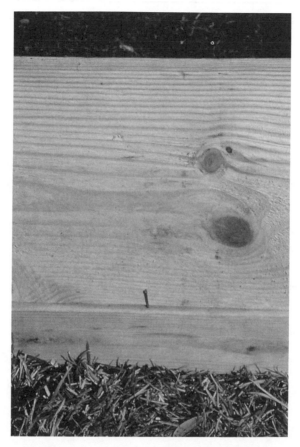

Small nails, strategically located, will prevent the 2 × 12 frame from sliding around on the 2 × 4 foundation during positioning and filling.

Whichever way you choose, now comes the fun part: filling the boxes. If you have never gardened before, you cannot appreciate what a wonderful opportunity it is to start from scratch and custom-mix a perfect garden soil. And I must tell you, it's a little like making bouillabaisse. There's no one recipe. You can throw in a bit of this, a bit of that. As a general rule, though,

I would recommend mixing about one part sand, two parts topsoil, and one part organic matter.

If you don't need much soil to fill your beds — for example, if you only need to fill four 4 × 4 foot frames six inches deep — you can probably get by, and save some money, by purchasing bags of sand, topsoil, fine bark mulch, and peat moss from a nursery. As a rough guide, six bags of sand, 12 bags of topsoil, one bag of fine bark mulch, and half a bale of peat moss should suffice for one 4 × 4 bed that is 12 inches deep, though bag volumes vary.

If you need much more than that, you will want to order it from a landscaping company, who will sell it by the cubic yard. Since one cubic yard equals 27 cubic feet, if your beds are one foot deep, you will need one cubic yard of dirt for every 27 square feet of garden surface. You can order ready-mixed "sandy loam" (half sand, half topsoil), but be sure to order some topsoil to enrich it. Don't waste money on a landscaping company's "special garden mix" or similar concoction. It will probably be essentially sandy loam, plus a few chips of bark mulch.

You needn't purchase organic matter if you have a plentiful supply of compost, or if you own a shredder and have tree and shrub branches and leaves to mulch up. Don't use whole leaves — they take too long to decompose. Don't use grass clippings — they break down too rapidly. As you fill your boxes, pour a layer of each substance at a time, blending the different substances with your hands every few inches.

And when you're done, what you will have created is the perfect growing medium for vegetable plants, as well as a soil blend that will be easy to work, with nothing more than your fingers, year after year. One nice bonus from the wooden frames: it's easy to nail on stakes and trellises. (A simple trellis can be constructed from two vertical 1 × 1 sticks, with horizontal 1 × 1's attached at one foot intervals.) With time (about one growing season), the wood will age gracefully into a bleached gray, at which point your boxes will cease looking like fresh pine coffins and blend nicely into the natural environment.

PLANNING THE GARDEN

Planning what to plant where and when is the most dynamic aspect of vegetable gardening. Each winter, you should draw up a "master plan" for the following growing season. Nothing fancy, mind you. You can do it in an hour if your garden is small and you are one of those people with common sense who make fast decisions. It takes me *several* hours. Every weekend. My master plan is always changing.

First, list the things you would like to grow that year. Then, prioritize them, "1" being the vegetable you would most like to grow, and so forth. Next, draw the outline of your garden beds on a piece of graph paper. Then start filling in those empty squares, beginning with your top priorities.

Your main considerations in siting crops should be how much space each will require (consider both plant diameter and how many plants you will need), how tall each will get (remember, you want taller plants to the north, shorter plants to the south), and what you grew in each bed last year (you want to rotate, if possible).

For new gardeners, the space and height information can be obtained from the vegetable information chart in this chapter. Also, be sure to read specific sections on specific vegetables, later in this book. Plant sizes will vary, depending on variety, climate, weather, how closely you plant, and whether you use stakes, trellises, or cages for some plants.

Another consideration is appearance. I like my garden to be attractive as well as functional. You may want to allocate a prominent location to red lettuce. You might take into account that bush squash tends to look weedy and unkempt late in life. Another tactic is to group things that do most of their growing during the same time frame altogether. That way you always have some beds that are full — a "garden for all seasons."

Do you have space left? (I usually do, at this point) If so, think of some other things you might like to grow just for fun. A novelty plant, perhaps. Flowers. Something that looks neat. Something you haven't eaten in years.

Or did you run out of space before exhausting your list? If so, consider whether any of the vegetables you selected lend themselves to "succession cropping." To make the most efficient use of space (and not have boring-looking bare spots in your garden for long), you will want to follow up short-lived spring crops with summer, or "main season" crops. When summer crops are done, you may want to follow up with fall crops, which generally are the same ones grown in spring.

Commonly grown cool-weather crops, which do best in spring or fall in most areas, include:

broccoli	onions
Brussels sprouts	peas
carrots	potatoes
cauliflower	radishes
collard greens	spinach
lettuce	turnips

Many of the above vegetables will grow all summer in especially cool climates like the Rockies or south-central Alaska. Some will grow all *winter* in especially *warm* areas, such as the deep South.

Main-season crops (that may not do well at all in very cool climates) include:

beans	peppers
cantaloupes	pumpkins
corn	squash
cucumbers	sweet potatoes
eggplant	tomatoes
okra	watermelons

Succession cropping can force some hard decisions. In some cases, a "spring" crop is not really done until early or midsummer, which may be too

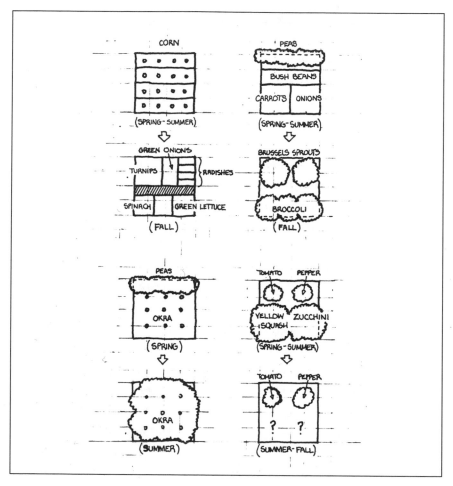

Garden layout, drawn on graph paper, with transitions for succession cropping. Scale: 1 square on paper = 1 square foot in garden.

late to get much production out of a summer crop. Or a "summer" crop may still be producing well in fall, when you're ready to plant cool-weather stuff again. You simply have to decide which crops are more important to you. You may decide to remove a crop early or plant one late, either of which will sacrifice some production. In some segments of your garden, you may want to follow up spring crops directly with fall crops, after a short time-out during summer. Obviously, the longer your growing season, the easier and more logical succession cropping is. Gardeners in mild climate areas will likely want a succession of garden plans — e.g., one each for spring, summer, and fall — rather than just one. In fact, gardening can be never-ending in an area like the California coast.

Next, figure out optimum planting and transplanting dates for each crop for your area. This information likewise can be calculated from the vegetable chart and the later sections on specific vegetables. An additional bit of information you must know, however, is when the last freezing temperatures ("frost") normally occur in spring and when frost normally resumes in fall. This, of course, varies by region. To assist you, this chapter includes two maps and one table on the subject. If your city is not listed in the climatological table, or if you live "on a line" on the maps, find a city that's close or "split the difference." Interpolation or extrapolation will work very well for the large, flat, landlocked majority of the U.S. It can be tricky, however, around mountains, coasts, and the Great Lakes.

An even more reliable source for planting dates would be a local one, such as a newspaper gardening column or state agriculture department extension office. Usually a range of dates is provided for planting a particular crop. All else being equal, it's best not to plant at the earliest or latest dates in those ranges, as that means that you're taking a chance it will be too cold or too hot for a given plant to do its best.

Now it's time to get out the calendar, and make up a planting schedule, in chronological order. If you work weekdays and garden on weekends, you might as well make every date on your list a weekend.

For seedlings started indoors, there will be about two weeks of lost time for "acclimatizing," during which little growth will occur. These two weeks are already figured into the "WEEKS TO TRANSPLANT" column in the Vegetable Guide. For example, tomato plants require about six weeks from seed-

FROST DATA FOR SELECTED LOCATIONS

Location	Last Frost		First Frost	
	Average	90% Safe	10% Chance	Average
Albuquerque	MAY 12	MAY 26	SEP 25	OCT 9
Anchorage	MAY 4	MAY 15	SEP 10	SEP 25
Asheville NC	APR 10	APR 24	OCT 11	OCT 24
Atlanta	APR 7	APR 21	OCT 14	OCT 29
Baltimore-Washington	APR 13	APR 27	OCT 14	OCT 31
Bangor ME	MAY 24	JUN 8	SEP 7	SEP 19
Billings MT	MAY 12	MAY 29	SEP 6	SEP 23
Birmingham AL	MAR 31	APR 16	OCT 20	NOV 3
Bismark ND	MAY 14	MAY 26	SEP 7	SEP 20
Boston	APR 26	MAY 12	OCT 3	OCT 16
Buffalo	APR 29	MAY 14	OCT 4	OCT 21
Burlington VT	MAY 11	MAY 25	SEP 19	OCT 1
Charleston	MAR 18	APR 6	OCT 30	NOV 12
Chatanooga	APR 5	APR 18	OCT 19	NOV 1
Chicago	APR 22	MAY 6	OCT 10	OCT 23
Cincinnati	APR 21	MAY 5	OCT 5	OCT 19
Cleveland	APR 27	MAY 12	OCT 8	OCT 23
Dallas-Ft Worth	MAR 23	APR 9	OCT 27	NOV 13
Des Moines	APR 28	MAY 11	SEP 24	OCT 7
Detroit	APR 27	MAY 12	OCT 5	OCT 19
Denver	MAY 7	MAY 23	SEP 17	OCT 4
Fairbanks AK	MAY 17	MAY 25	AUG 24	SEP 5
Honolulu	—	—	—	—
Houston	FEB 15	MAR 13	NOV 20	DEC 14
Jacksonville FL	FEB 14	MAR 14	NOV 8	NOV 29
Kansas City	APR 18	MAY 2	OCT 3	OCT 18
Las Vegas	MAR 7	APR 3	NOV 7	NOV 21
Little Rock	MAR 25	APR 9	OCT 24	NOV 5
Los Angeles	—	FEB 3	JAN 1	—
Louisville	APR 20	MAY 6	OCT 6	OCT 20

FROST DATA FOR SELECTED LOCATIONS

Location	Last Frost Average	Last Frost 90% Safe	First Frost 10% Chance	First Frost Average
Miami	—	—	—	—
Memphis	MAR 23	APR 8	OCT 27	NOV 7
Milwaukee	MAY 4	MAY 18	SEP 26	OCT 11
Minneapolis-St Paul	MAY 7	MAY 19	SEP 15	SEP 30
Mobile	FEB 27	MAR 19	NOV 5	NOV 26
Nashville	APR 5	APR 16	OCT 14	OCT 29
New Orleans	FEB 20	MAR 21	NOV 15	DEC 5
New York City	APR 1	APR 13	OCT 27	NOV 11
Norfolk VA	MAR 23	APR 6	OCT 31	NOV 17
Oklahoma City	APR 4	APR 17	OCT 18	OCT 31
Omaha	APR 27	MAY 11	SEP 25	OCT 9
Orlando	JAN 24	FEB 28	DEC 4	JAN 3
Philadelphia	APR 15	APR 28	OCT 14	OCT 27
Phoenix	FEB 5	MAR 16	NOV 18	DEC 15
Pittsburgh	MAY 1	MAY 18	SEP 28	OCT 13
Portland OR	APR 3	APR 26	OCT 18	NOV 7
Raleigh-Durham NC	APR 11	APR 29	OCT 16	OCT 27
Richmond	APR 10	APR 27	OCT 13	OCT 26
St Louis	APR 16	MAY 1	OCT 6	OCT 21
Salt Lake City	MAY 10	MAY 27	SEP 23	OCT 7
San Antonio	MAR 3	MAR 23	NOV 6	NOV 24
San Fransisco-Oakland	JAN 23	FEB 15	DEC 1	DEC 29
Seattle	MAR 24	APR 20	OCT 27	NOV 11
Spokane	MAY 4	MAY 20	SEP 19	OCT 5
Topeka KA	APR 21	MAY 4	OCT 1	OCT 14
Tuscon	FEB 25	MAR 29	NOV 7	NOV 30

NOTE: Data derived from statistics provided by National Climatic Data Center, Asheville, NC. For larger metropolitan areas, where possible, temperatures shown are averages, based on statistics from several weather stations over a broad area, e.g., downtown, suburbs, airports. In some instances, variation within areas can be significant, particularly near mountains, oceans, or the Great Lakes.

ing to reach appropriate transplant size, but you must start them eight weeks before the optimum transplant date, to allow for "hardening."

I'm afraid I'm making all this sound somewhat simpler than it really is, especially for a beginning gardener. There is only so much advice to give you, however. This is one of those aspects of gardening in which you call the shots, and nobody else can make the decisions for you. Still, if you're a gardener you will find a way to sort it all out and have fun doing it. If you're not, you might as well find that out early on.

If you have a home computer, that's the place to keep your garden notes. I start a new file each year, titled simply "GARDEN 199–." You needn't make a chore out of it, but every couple of weeks sit down for a few minutes and record any experiences you might want to recall in subsequent years. For example, did your fall spinach fail to germinate because you planted it while temperatures were still too hot? How many carrot seeds did you sow, and over how big an area? Did too many come up, making extra work in thinning? Did your corn emerge only to die back during a week of hard frost? It may have been an unusual year, or you may want to plant corn two weeks later next time. Keep track of weather patterns. When did the first and last frosts occur? If you live in a suburb, fall frost may come earlier than downtown. What were the high and low daily temperatures like in April and May? Enter your planting schedule, and keep notes that will help you adjust it the next year. I find computer notes especially helpful over the winter, when I'm planning my next year's garden. At a minimum, they help you remember what you planted where, to facilitate crop rotation.

However, when it comes to struggling over what to plant where and when *this year*, nothing beats pencil and paper. After all your revisions are complete (you wanna bet?), you should wind up with two "documents":

– a garden layout, drawn on graph paper
– a chronological planting list.

Your final task is to list the types of seed you will need to order.

VEGETABLE GUIDE

Vegetable	Spacing Diameter (inches)₁	Height (inches)	Preferred Weather	Seed Depth (inches)	Days to Germinate
Beans, bush	3	9–24	warm	1 1/2	7–14
Beans, pole	4	72	warm	1 1/2	7–14
Broccoli	18	24	cool	1/2	7–14
Brussels Sprouts	18–24	24–30	cool	1/2	7–14
Cantaloupes	24–30	—	warm	1	5–10
Carrots	2–3	18–24	cool-warm	1/4–1/2	14–21
Cauliflower	18–24	24	cool	1/2	7–14
Chard	6–12	12	all	1	7–14
Collards	12–18	12–18	cool	1/2	7–14
Corn	12	60–84	warm	2	7–10
Cucumbers	24	—	warm	2	7–10
Eggplant	18–24	18–30	warm	1/2	10–14
Lettuce, leaf	6	6	cool	1/4	7–14
Okra	18–24	60–90	warm–hot	1	7–14
Onions, long day (sets)	1 1/2–5	24	cool	2	7–14
Onions, short day (seeds)	1–5	24	cool	1/2	7–14
Peas	2	72	cool	2	7–14
Peppers	15–24	18–36	warm	1/4–1/2	14–21
Potato, Irish	12–18	18–24	cool	3–6	14–30
Pumpkin	30–36	—	warm	1–2	7–10
Radishes	1 1/2–2	3	cool	1/2	7–14
Rutabaga	6–12	6–12	cool	1/2	7–14
Spinach	6	4	cool	1/2	7–14
Squash	24	24 (bush)	warm	1	7–10
Sweet Potato	12–18	15	hot	—	—
Tomato	18–24	24–48 (caged)	warm	1/2	7–10
Turnips	3–4	4–6	cool	1/2	7–14
Watermelon	30–36	—	warm	1	6–10

Zucchini

VEGETABLE GUIDE

Weeks to Transplant[2]	Days to Maturity	Frost Tolerance	Optimum Time to Plant/Transplant Spring[3]	Fall[4]	Length of Harvest (weeks)	# of "Fruit" Per Plant
—	45–60	none	+2–6	—	2–3	5–15
—	60–75	none	+2–6	—	X	10–25
8	60–90	slight	−4–6	−10–13	3–4	1–5
8	90	moderate	−4–6	−10–13	4	25–50
4	90	none	+2–6	—	X	3–5
—	60–90	moderate	−4	−12	2–4	1
8	60–90	slight	−4–6	−10–13	1	1
—	60	slight	−4–?	−?–12	X	—
8	60	slight	−4	−10–13	4–8	—
—	70–90	none	0–+4	—	1	2
4	60	none	+2–4	—	X	20–50
10	75–90	none	+2–4	—	X	5–10
6	45–60	slight	−3–0	−8–10	3–6	—
—	50–60	none	+3–6	—	X	20–100
—	120*	moderate	−4–6	−8–10**	1–4	1
—	150–210***	moderate	−4–6**	−4–6	1–4	1
—	60–75	slight	−2–6	—	2–4	10–25
10	75–90	none	+2–6	—	X	10–50
—	90–120	slight	−4	−14–16	—	5–10
4	85–110	none	0–+4	−12–16	1–2	2–5
—	30–45	slight	−4–0	−6–8	1	1
—	75–90	slight	−3–5	—	1–3	1
8	45–60	moderate	−4	−4–8	4–6	—
4	45–60	none	0–+4	—	4–6	10–20
12	120	none	+4–6	—	—	5–10
8	60–80	none	+2–6	—	X	15–30
—	45–60	slight	1 2	−6–10	1–2	1
4	75–90	none	+3–6	—	X	4–6

[1] Space to allow for roots. Top growth may vary. [2] Includes two weeks for "hardening." [3] Number of Weeks before (−) or after (+) average last frost. [4] Number of weeks before (−) average first frost. * Green onions 45–75 days. ** For green onions only. *** Green onions 60–90 days. X Will grow all summer in most places.

AVERAGE DATE OF FIRST FROST IN FALL

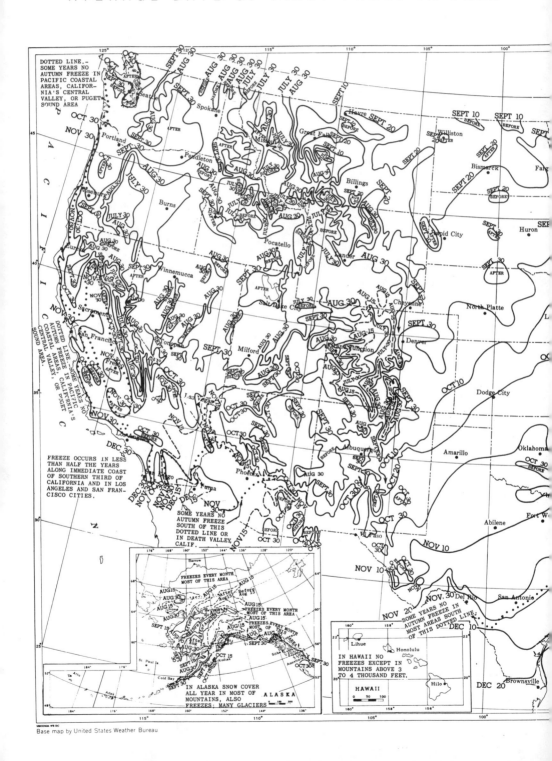

"BEFORE" OR "AFTER" IS ENTERED ON MOST SMALL
AREAS OF THIS MAP TO SHOW MORE READILY
WHETHER THE MEAN FREEZE DATE IN THE AREA IS
BEFORE OR AFTER THE DATE PRINTED ON THE
LINE.

AUTUMN (FALL) FREEZES ARE ASSUMED TO OCCUR
BETWEEN JULY 1 AND DECEMBER 31.

CAUTION SHOULD BE USED IN INTERPOLATING ON
THIS GENERALIZED MAP. SHARP CHANGES IN THE
MEAN DATE MAY OCCUR IN SHORT DISTANCES, DUE
TO DIFFERENCES IN ALTITUDE, SLOPE OF LAND,
TYPE OF SOIL, VEGETATIVE COVER, BODIES OF
WATER, AIR DRAINAGE, URBAN HEAT EFFECTS,
ETC.

AVERAGE DATE OF LAST FROST IN SPRING

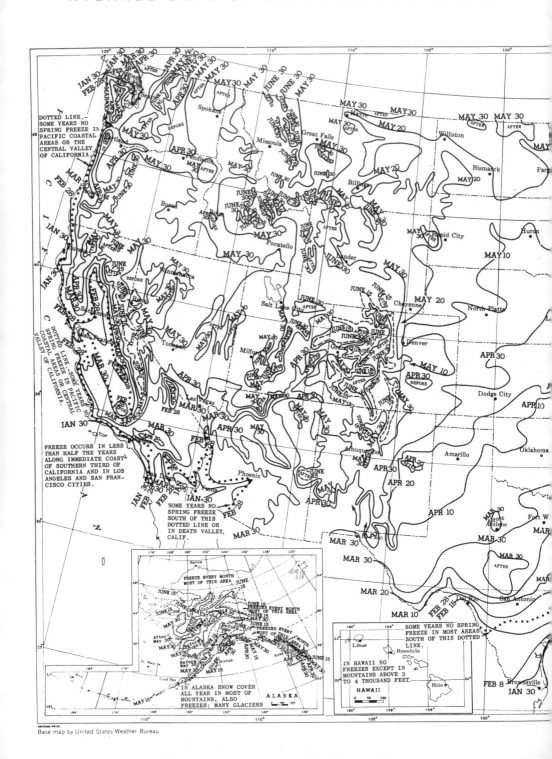

SEEDS

Buying seed is not something to be done casually. If you care enough about vegetable gardens to have one, then you owe it to yourself to be pretty picky about what goes in it. We gardeners go to a lot of trouble perfecting our soil, fertilizing, watering, staking, pruning, killing insects, insuring optimum light conditions...but then to up and plant any old generic seed just because some discount store was unloading a bunch for 15 cents a packet ... After all, the seed you select is the single most important factor determining what kind of plant you'll have and vegetables you'll harvest.

There are so many varieties of seed to choose from nowadays that you can achieve almost any aim. Are you after taste? Size? Novel color? Fast maturity? A robust plant that resists disease? A small plant that won't take up too much of your bed? A warm-weather plant that does well in cool climates? All else being equal, I buy the cheapest seed. But seldom is all else equal.

You can buy vegetable seeds almost anywhere, of course, including local nurseries and discount department stores. Their selections are limited, however. What's more, they are biased toward the "average" taste. Which means you'll have trouble finding the biggest or the tastiest or the fastest. Instead, you'll find good all-around seeds that produce "pretty good" fruit on "pretty healthy" plants in most parts of the country.

Order from seed catalogs. You'll be able to get exactly what you want, and even if some of the things you want *are* ordinary "all-around" varieties, the mail order companies have those too. Besides, it's fun looking through the catalogs over the winter. The best-known seed company is probably Burpee, although I've always found Park Seed to be equally "big-time" and reliable. Gardening magazines usually have tear-out postcards each fall that you can mail to various seed companies to receive their free catalogs, or you can simply write a letter. All of the following companies are large, reputable, national in scope — and have been around a long time:

W. Atlee Burpee & Co.
021832 Burpee Bldg.
P.O. Box 5114
Warminster, PA 18974

Henry Field's Seed & Nursery Co.
415 N. Burnett
Shenandoah, IA 51602

Gurney Seed & Nursery Co.
110 Capital St.
Yankton, SD 57079

Harris Seeds
P.O. Box 22960
Rochester, NY 14692

Park Seed Co.
Cokesbury Rd.
P.O. Box 46
Greenwood, SC 29648

Stokes Seeds Inc.
1333 Stokes Bldg.
P.O. Box 548
Buffalo, NY 14240

All the above cater to home gardeners, except for Stokes, which is some-what slanted toward the farm trade — e.g., tomatoes that can be picked green for shipping but still have good-quality flesh after ripening (however, Stokes sometimes has seeds you can't find anywhere else). In addition, there are many fine small- to mid-sized companies around the country that specialize in regional markets, "heirloom," gourmet, oriental, etc.

Regional varieties are ones that have been bred specially to withstand extreme heat, cold, or moisture conditions. Heirlooms are traditional, genetically unimproved varieties, which have not been specially bred with any purpose in mind. An heirloom tomato might be identical to one eaten by Thomas Jefferson! If you have no other reason to select a particular seed, I would recommend the varieties Park labels "High Performers," the ones Burpee puts the bullseye symbol on, or ones advertised as recent award winners.

Many seeds are hybrids. Crossing two varieties often results in the most desirable traits. Eventually, some crosses "breed true," in which case they are customarily no longer identified as hybrids. If you grow a genuine hybrid, however, and save seed from the fruit it produces, the second generation may not be the same variety, depending on genetic luck. Nonetheless, some of my best tomatoes were grown on plants that came up wild in the compost pile!

I do save originally purchased seed from year to year and use the same packets until they're empty (I throw nothing out, as long as it still works). When I'm done planting, I roll the packets up as airtight as possible, wrap a rubber band around several such packs, and slip the whole bunch into a zip-lock bag. Throw in a rolled-up tissue containing a teaspoon of baby powder (also secured with a rubber band) as a dessicant, and try to squeeze the air out of the zip-lock bag before sealing. Then stick it in the back of the refrigerator, behind the soft drinks, until you need some seed again. Cared for in this manner, most seeds will last for years. On the other hand, stored open, in a damp basement or hot garage, seeds may not be good for two years running; this is especially true for corn, pea, and bean seed.

If you "re-use" your seed like I do, that's all the more reason to be careful in your selection to start with ... and all the less reason to niggle over a few cents difference in price. Incidentally, one problem I *haven't* often encountered is "bad" seed. Theoretically, seed that has been stored in hot or damp warehouses before wholesaling to retail outlets might not have a very high germination rate. Seed from disreputable suppliers might be diseased or from last year's crop. However, I haven't found any of these problems to be common, whether buying from one of the well-known seed companies or from a mass merchandiser.

When planting seeds, a good rule of thumb is to plant at a depth equal to five times the seed's diameter. Most seeds germinate best in loose, lightly packed, moist (not wet) soil. The one exception is spinach, which sprouts best in slightly drier soil. When seeds are planted directly in the garden, the soil should be moistened daily. Late afternoon is best, because the soil will stay moist all night and still be slightly damp all morning, but the couple of hours of sunlight remaining after watering will dry the soil *surface* enough to prevent fungus.

Do not follow such traditional seed packet advice as "sow at a rate of one per inch, then thin after emergence to a spacing of six inches." It's a waste of seed (the seed companies, after all, *want* you to use a lot of seeds) and also makes for extra work (if you don't enjoy weeding, why would you enjoy thinning?). Instead, as a general rule, where I want one plant, I sow one seed. I may sow one extra, just in case. Exceptions are onions and carrots, whose germination rates are lower and for which it would be far too tedious to plant one seed every place you want one plant. Those seeds are best "broadcast."

Tomato, pepper, eggplant, and cabbage family seed are started indoors, in small pots, in order to get a jump on the growing season. I prefer to start lettuce and spinach the same way.

SEEDLINGS

I can't imagine purchasing transplants from a nursery. I always start my own. It's not snobbery. Starting your own is the only way to get most varieties, since nurseries offer a limited selection. It's also cheaper. And, assuming you do it right, you'll have healthier, prettier plants. But probably the most important reason I start my own transplants is that I like to grow things. That's why I garden. And the most fun part of growing things is the magic of converting a speck of dried up seed into a beautiful, healthy plant. To simply pick up and continue growing something someone else already grew the best part of is akin to heating up a frozen pie.

Start tomatoes, spinach, and cabbage family members eight weeks before the desired transplant date; peppers and eggplants ten; and lettuce six. This allows two weeks for acclimatizing, during which little growth normally occurs. All can get by with somewhat less time, however, so if something goes wrong and the seeds don't sprout, there will still be time to replant. Once plants have been in the garden a month, it's hard to tell the difference between one that was started "on schedule" and one that began life two weeks later.

The simplest and cheapest "seed starting kit" is a package of styrofoam coffee cups and some sort of plastic tray you can put them in for "bottom watering" (look for refrigerator vegetable trays in the houseware section of a discount department store). The cups can be reused for several years if you're careful. The trays will last forever. The cups hold more soil than commercial seed-starting kits, which means bigger root balls and healthier plants, off to a faster start. (When it's time to transplant, root balls will slide out easily if you turn the plants upside down and apply a little pressure to the bottom of the cup.)

Using a pencil, punch three evenly spaced holes, about a quarter inch in diameter, around the base of each cup — on the side, just above the bottom. The holes will allow drainage and, equally important, will allow your seedlings to suck up water from the bottom, leaving the soil surface undisturbed.

Fill the cups with potting soil, and pack lightly. You needn't purchase fancy "starter" mix. Most ordinary potting soils work fine. But do avoid one

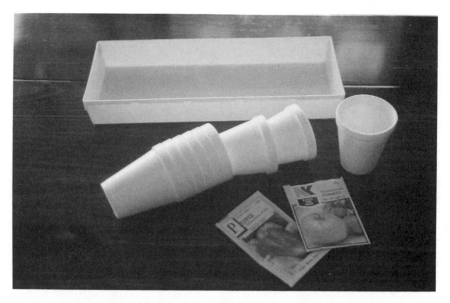

The simplest and cheapest ''seed-starting kit'' consists of
styrofoam coffee cups and a plastic tray for bottom watering.

Punch holes near the bottoms of the cups.

A pencil is the most useful "tool" for indoor seed sowing.

unusual type that consists of finely ground pine needles and bark, as it tends to crust and prevent seed germination.

For home-started seedlings, most seeds are planted at a depth of 1/4 to 1/2 inch. Poke a hole in the soil surface, near the center, with the point of a pencil, drop a seed in, poke it down gently with the pencil point, and firm the soil moderately to close the hole. Plant two seeds per cup, just in case, although both seeds will sprout most of the time. Occasionally, neither will germinate, and you will have to replant.

Seeds need fairly firm soil contact to sprout properly. A seed sends down a root first. Then the stem forms between the root and seed, eventually poking up above the soil surface in an inverted U, while the seed remains buried. The growing stem now pulls the germinal leaves out of the seedcase, while the soil holds the case down beneath the surface. If the soil is not firm enough or the seed is not planted deep enough, the growing stem will pull the entire seed out of the soil and the leaves will not pop out.

Don't forget to number each styrofoam cup (a ballpoint pen provides the most durable identification) as you plant it. And be sure to keep a "key" — in fact, two copies, to be safe. Otherwise, come transplant time, beginning gardeners may not know a pepper from a tomato, and even veterans won't be able to tell a cherry tomato from a beefsteak.

It's a good idea to plant a few extra pots, in case one of your seedlings turns out unhealthy or doesn't survive transplanting. However, this is seldom a problem if you do things right. If you want three tomato plants, you may want to start four. If you want three different types of tomato plant, you could start two of each, or consider just planting one extra, of the type that is most important to you. I virtually never use my extras and usually wind up giving them away after I know my transplants are going to make it. That, too, is allowed (it's my garden).

After seeds are planted, put the styrofoam cups in the plastic tray and fill the tray with an inch of water. Let the pots soak up water for a couple of hours, until the soil surfaces are damp. Then, if any water remains in the bottom of the tray, temporarily remove the pots and dump out the excess. Do not let the pots stand in water indefinitely, especially while waiting for seeds to sprout, as that will cause the soil to be too mucky for germination.

Most seeds should germinate in about a week, although peppers require about two. If your seedlings aren't up by then, don't be alarmed — it could take up to a week longer — but, to save time, go ahead and replant. Sow two more seeds per cup, nearer the edge of the cup this time, so as not to mess up the ones you planted earlier if they're still viable.

Most seeds sprout best at about 80 degrees Fahrenheit. But don't try to get too fancy, such as putting the tray on a heating pad. It could backfire and make the soil too hot. Room temperature is fine. Anyway, heating elements are expensive to operate. Seeds *will* sprout in an environment somewhat cooler than room temperature, but it takes longer. A basement or garage may be *too* cool.

Water whenever the soil surfaces seem dry and the pots feel light (about twice a week). After most of the seedlings are up, begin using a balanced liquid fertilizer (such as 10–10–10) every other time you water. You needn't go to a lot of trouble mixing fertilizer solutions. Simply put a few drops in the bottom of the tray, and add water; it will mix itself. Also, once seedlings are up, make sure the soil surface is *good and dry* before watering. This forces roots to grow deep and also prevents fungus on the soil surface, which occasionally can cause "damping off" and kill a plant.

You will need a grow light, at least after the seedlings start coming up. I don't care what anybody says—even a "sunny" window won't provide enough light for seedlings to do well (besides that, it's cold by the window). The minimum you will need is one 24-inch-long fluorescent light fixture that holds two bulbs. For most gardeners, a 48-inch two-bulb fixture would be better, as it will, obviously, accommodate more plants. You can mount the fixture under a kitchen cupboard, suspended from two chains attached to hooks screwed into the cabinet bottom, which will enable you to raise and lower the light to the optimum distance from the plants. If you're the least bit handy, you can easily build a lighted plant stand for under $50 that will be attractive enough to be around other furniture. Or you can buy one ready-made for $300–400 (are they crazy or what?)! You can buy a small, ready-made mini-stand, with one 24-inch bulb, for about $50.

Grow light bulbs are slightly more effective than ordinary fluorescent bulbs, but either will work. Keep the light one to two inches from the tops of the plants, even though that may sound too close. Provide 14 hours of light a day, using a timer. Give your seedlings a rest at night, because continuous light 24 hours a day burns leaves and stunts growth. As the plants grow, you will have to gradually raise the light. If you find that your seedlings vary in size significantly, put the taller ones on one end, shorter ones on the other, and hang the light at an angle.

A grow light is essential for starting your own seedlings.

Homemade lighted plant stand.

"HARDENING OFF" TECHNIQUES

Home-started seedlings need about two weeks of "hardening off" before transplanting. Otherwise, they will never survive the shock of full sun and wind (novice seedling starters especially underestimate the significance of the latter) in the garden. Find a spot outdoors that gets sun for only half a day, or 50% filtered shade throughout the day, and where about two thirds of the wind is blocked.

Again, I don't care what anybody says, one week of hardening is not enough. Two weeks is about right. And if the weather cooperates, start hardening your plants *three or four* weeks before you intend to transplant. On a warm, sunny spring day, seedlings will grow just as well on the deck or patio as they would under a grow light.

Common advice is to gradually expose plants to increasing amounts of sun, wind, and temperature extremes. This graduated approach is not necessary. And it's out and out *harmful* if done too fast (which it almost always is). Abide by the "KISS" principle (Keep It Simple, Stupid): Find yourself a spot where half of the sun and two thirds of the wind are blocked. Put your seedlings there. Leave them there for two weeks.

DO bring your plants in at night, however. Even if there's no danger of frost. It's always colder at night, and in the spring, when hardening is usually accomplished, it's almost always much colder than optimum for tomatoes and peppers. Seedlings brought in at night grow more than ones that are left outside 24 hours a day. In fact, the latter, likely as not, won't grow at all. And don't be afraid to bring your plants in occasionally on an exceptionally cold, rainy, or windy *day* and put them back under the grow light. That's why plants have gardeners.

The purpose of hardening is to get plants accustomed to sun and wind, not cold or heat. Plants already know what to do in warm air; they need not be prepared for it gradually. And they already know they don't like cold air.

Once in the garden, they will seldom be exposed to cold, and when they are, it will not help to have been exposed to it before. There is nothing to be gained from teaching your plants how to suffer.

3

THE
VEGETABLES

BEANS AND PEAS

The bean and pea family is quite a varied group. Consider: string beans (green or yellow), lima beans, pinto and kidney beans, navy beans, garbanzo beans, English peas, snow peas, black-eyed peas (for gardening purposes, consider it a bean), sugar snap peas ... Yet, they have much in common, too. They are all "legumes," which is to say, they come in pods and return nitrogen to the soil. They are all planted and grown similarly, and the plants themselves look similar, except that almost all peas grow on vines, while beans are readily available in both bush *and* vine (or "pole") varieties. Another difference is that peas like cool weather; beans like it warm.

Beans and peas are hardy, attractive plants that do well in average garden soil. Beans can be planted any time after the average last frost date. Peas must be planted at least a couple of weeks before the average last frost date, in order to get maximum production before hot weather kills them. The bean

61

and pea varieties most commonly grown in backyard vegetable gardens today are green, or string, beans and "sugar peas." The latter is a fairly new class of sweet, plump, crunchy pods that started with Sugar Snap in the 1970's.

A 2 × 4 foot patch of bush beans should be adequate for a family of two to four. When planting, crumble up the soil with your hands, adding some compost, and level the dirt off about 1 1/2–2 inches shy of the top of your raised bed frame. This will require temporarily removing some soil or pushing it aside. Cover the patch with seed, at about 3–4-inch intervals in all directions. You need not make orderly, squared-off rows, as they won't be apparent once the plants are growing anyway. Next, cover the seed bed with about 1–1 1/2 inches of the dirt you removed. Sprinkle on 5–10–10 fertilizer, at a rate of half a cup for a 2 × 4 patch. Add another half inch of dirt, to keep the fertilizer from washing away. Pat it all down moderately. Then, if you like, add a half inch of fine bark mulch. Finally, moisten the soil to a depth of 4–5 inches, using a sprinkler or nozzle set on fine mist.

Moisten daily, preferably in late afternoon, until germination, which takes about a week if the weather is warm, but up to two weeks if the temperature is less than ideal. You should not need to thin bush beans. A few will probably not sprout. Bugs may eat a few while they're small. And an eventual average spacing of 4–5 inches is about right. I have tried planting a few extras, somewhere else in the garden, to transplant into any bare spots in my "bean bed," but they suffer a setback during transplanting, due to the fact that they already have quite extensive root systems by the time they reach two to three inches' height. The transplants lag behind the others in growth, and soon get shaded out by the others.

In a raised bed full of good soil, bush beans will grow to 18–24 inches' height. Expect to pick your first beans 45–60 days after planting. Pods are best picked slightly immature, before the seeds begin to bulge inside the shells. Bush beans produce over several weeks, and then die. But don't be too hasty in removing them. Sometimes you get a week or two of production, fol-

An easy way to plant bush beans is to remove a layer of soil, lay
the seed down, then cover with the soil you removed.

lowed by a week's rest, then another week of production. You may want several staggered plantings, in order to extend the harvest (unless you live in an
extremely hot or cold climate, in which case you want to concentrate your
planting, to take full advantage of the brief suitable growing seasons).

Pole beans — and almost all *peas* — should be grown on trellises, which you
can nail to your wooden raised bed frame. A five-foot-high trellis eight feet
wide (or two four-foot-wide trellises, in separate beds) should feed a family of
two to four. At planting time, crumble up the soil and add humus along the
trellis(es) out to a width of nine inches. Then, with your finger, form a 1 1/2
–2-inch-deep trench through the soil along the trellis. Drop a seed in every
two inches for peas, every four inches for beans. Close the trench. Sprinkle a
half cup of 5–10–10 (for an eight-foot row) along the sealed trench, and
work it into the top inch of soil. Mulch, if you like, and water like bush beans.

Pole beans and peas produce fewer pods at a time, but over an extended period. Pole beans will provide more pounds of produce, per square foot of soil, than bush beans.

Pea quality will decline as the weather warms, until, finally, the plants themselves start to decline. When you remove bean and pea vines, do chop them up and dig them into the garden. The dead roots, in particular, enrich the soil with nitrogen for an appropriate follow-on crop, such as corn or greens.

THE CABBAGE FAMILY

The cabbage, or cole, family includes broccoli, Brussels sprouts, cauliflower, collards (or "collard greens"), kale, and kohlrabi, as well as, of course, "ordinary" cabbage. All prefer cool weather. In America, the most commonly grown are broccoli, Brussels sprouts, and cauliflower. All three are normally started indoors for spring or fall transplanting.

Seeds are planted at a half-inch depth. Allow six weeks from seeding to reach optimum transplant size, plus two weeks for acclimatizing, or a total of eight weeks. Spring crops are transplanted about a month before the average last frost date. Fall crops are transplanted about three months before the average first frost. All cole crops will survive some mild frost, which often even improves the taste.

Allow 18–24 inches between plants, and expect them to reach a similar height. Average soil is fine, but mix a little compost into the soil before planting. Bury each transplant about 1/4–1/2-inch deeper than its previous soil line in the styrofoam cup. Then, using your fingers, mix a fourth cup of 15–10–10 fertilizer into the top inch of soil around each plant, out to a radius of six inches, being careful not to get any on the plant itself. For Brussels sprouts, refertilize after six weeks, applying half a cup out to a nine-inch radius.

Broccoli is undoubtedly the most popular of the "big three." Each plant will produce one large head, 60–90 days (depending on the variety and the weather) after transplanting, followed by several smaller heads. If allowed to continue (if the weather cooperates), you will get increasingly tiny heads, which really aren't worth fooling with. That's the time to remove the plants. Harvest the main heads when they're about normal grocery-store-broccoli size, before individual buds in the heads start showing definition and *well before* buds start turning into little yellow flowers.

Brussels sprouts are the most cold-tolerant plants of the three, as well as the most unusual looking. The heads form all along the trunk. (The same neighbor who planted 100 tomato plants kept removing "these funny-looking growths" that kept appearing on the trunks of his Brussels sprouts.) To help the "sprouts" reach maximum size, remove the plant's lower leaves (not the sprouts), which concentrates the plant's energy on producing sprouts, not foliage. As the plant gets taller, continue removing leaves up the trunk, always leaving perhaps a half dozen large leaves and an equal number of small ones on top for photosynthesis. Expect to pluck your first sprouts about 90 days after transplanting. Spring harvest can continue until summer heat starts affecting sprout quality (you will notice the heads opening up and leafing out). Fall harvest will continue until severe, continuous frost arrives.

Cauliflower, which matures in about 75 days, is the most trouble to grow. Or, at any rate, it *can* be. In order to keep the heads white and tender, "blanching" is required. That means that when the head starts forming you must pull the surrounding leaves over the head and tie them together, to keep the head in the dark. That's too much trouble for *my* garden! However, more and more gardeners are discovering that the *un*blanched cauliflower is just as tasty and nutritious as the blanched version. It simply turns out cream-colored. In some ways, I *prefer* it that way, as it seems more natural.

Collards are another cabbage-patch kid, especially popular among many Southerners. They are started and grown just like broccoli, Brussels sprouts, and cauliflower, and they require the same amount of room, but they are

Ornamental cabbage

somewhat more heat-tolerant. They don't head. You cook the leaves. For the tenderest greens and mildest flavor pick the leaves before they get too big. You can start harvesting at about 60 days.

One other cole family member I like to grow, even though you can't eat it, is ornamental, or flowering, cabbage. It is started indoors and grown just like all the other vegetables above. It will add color and fun to your vegetable garden.

REGIONAL CLIMATIC DIFFERENCES

In warmer areas, spring-grown Brussels sprouts do not do well, as it usually gets too warm too fast for tight, firm sprouts to develop. Stick to fall Brussels sprouts in such areas.

In all but the hottest climates, fall crops of all the above can be direct-seeded in the garden during summer, although they take up space you could be using for summer vegetables. I prefer transplants for both spring *and* fall. In very hot regions, cole seed will not germinate outdoors in the extreme summer heat.

In *very cool* areas, cole plants can be not just *seeded* but *grown* all summer.

CARROTS

When I was a kid, I never thought I would like to eat carrots. Carrots were "health food", appropriate only for the girl next door who wore support shoes and starched dresses. I'm not sure I ever ate one until I was 30 and started receiving them involuntarily in yuppie, nouvelle cuisine restaurants ("I'm Rob, I'll be your waiter, we have some specials this evening that aren't on the menu"), where we discovered that they were more than edible.

The first time I grew carrots it was just to try something different. I went for size. And succeeded. In getting giant, strong-smelling, overpowering-flavored roots. But God they were big. It took both hands and a strong back to extricate one from the dirt. While holding one's breath. They made impressive pictures. And they kept. For years. I also kept all the greens, because the books said you should do that: we boiled some and froze some and the refrigerator was full of them. The greens made especially good compost after they had decayed some in the crisper.

Then I tried growing baby gourmet, or "finger," carrots. They didn't im-
press the neighbors. We didn't keep the greens. But were they ever sweet,
mild, and indescribably delicious with an elegant meal and 8–10-year-old
French Burgundy. The best way to prepare them is the simplest way: pull,
rinse in cold water, steam (whole, just until slightly underdone), put a pat of
butter on each serving, and sprinkle with fresh-ground pepper. All carrots are
high in vitamins A and B, as well as calcium and phosphorous. But that's not
why you should eat your baby gourmets.

Carrots are easy to grow, and perfectly adapted to raised, intensive beds.
Follow these simple instructions, and I can almost guarantee you healthy
plants and a successful harvest. If you take my advice and grow baby
gourmets, I will also promise you of one of the most delightful vegetables
you'll ever eat.

First, select your seed. If you want finger carrots, don't try to grow a large
variety and simply pick some early. It's difficult to time, and they're not as

good. Baby gourmet types include Lady Finger, Little Finger, Baby Nantes, Baby Finger Nantes, and Baby Spike.

The best carrots are grown entirely "above ground," so if your raised-bed frame is only six inches deep, definitely stick with a finger variety. A two-foot by two-foot square should provide plenty for a family of two to four. Use a fairly sandy soil mix: about two parts sand, two parts topsoil, and one part soft, fine organic matter; peat moss or well-decayed compost works fine, but bark mulch may make the roots less than perfect. Blend the soil thoroughly, and pat it down gently. Then level the soil off one half inch shy of the top of the frame.

Here's a special seeding method, to insure optimum success. For a 4-square-foot planting, measure out approximately 300 seeds, plus or minus 25, on a kitchen plate. To get your 300 seeds, you needn't count them all. Instead, count out precisely 25 in a little pile, then eyeball another 11 piles of about equal size. Next, mix all the seed with one-fifth cup of "triple strength" (0–45–0) rock phosphate, in an empty spice container, such as red pepper flakes come in, with fairly large shaker holes on top. Then slowly sprinkle the mix, as evenly as possible, over the surface of your soil. The rock phosphate does two things: it makes it easier to distribute the seed evenly (the hardest aspect of sowing carrots), and it provides the single most important nutrient for growing good root crops (the less potent 0–15–0 and 0–30–0 rock phosphates act too slowly).

Next, mix up a blend of two parts topsoil, one part sand (no humus this time) in a bucket, and rubbing it slowly between the palms of your hands, sprinkle a layer approximately one-fourth-inch deep over the top of your seed. Do not use pure topsoil, as it tends to crust and prevent germination. Sprinkle one-half cup of 5–10–10 fertilizer (for a 2' × 2' patch) on top of the sandy loam layer. Then add one-eighth-inch more of the sandy loam mixture to keep the fertilizer from washing away. (The soil layer between seed and fertilizer "insulates" the seed from burn during germination.) Pat gently

Special carrot-seeding technique

again. Finally, mist the soil to a depth of about three inches, using a nozzle set on fine spray.

Mist the bed once daily, preferably in late afternoon, until the seeds sprout, which takes one to three weeks, depending on the temperature. You can anticipate about a 50% germination rate. Carrot seeds are planted several weeks before the average last frost date and will germinate in any temperature between 40 and 90 degrees Fahrenheit (70 seems to be ideal). Both seeds and seedlings will survive several mild frosts if they have to (in milder climates, where no extended hard frosts occur, carrots will grow all winter). After all have germinated that are going to, cut back watering to every other day and start watering deeper, but keep the spray fine so as not to damage the plants.

When your seedlings are an inch high, thin to a separation of 1–2 inches for finger carrots, 2 1/2–4 inches for larger varieties. Thinning is the only tedious part of growing carrots! After thinning, mulch with a half inch of fine bark mulch, being careful not to bury any plants. At this point, you can begin watering as you would anything else in your garden — deeply, gently, perhaps twice a week if you don't get rain. You won't need to fertilize again.

The seedlings you thin out can be transplanted to bare spots and will grow if you're careful, but most of them will turn out misshapen, with multiple trunks (good candidates for the Salad Shooter), because the tiny roots get damaged during transplanting and each broken spot tends to send out multiple new branches.

Carrots mature in 60–90 days. You can begin pulling baby gourmets when the tops are about nine inches high, which is considerably smaller than the greens on larger carrot varieties. If left in the ground longer, they will eventually approach smallish-normal carrot size but will still be excellent tasting. Larger varieties will grow tops up to 2 1/2 feet tall! If left longer than 90 days, they get increasingly strong flavored.

THE PERFECT METHOD FOR GROWING PERFECT SWEET CORN

Some evil things have happened to me while growing sweet corn. One year I had runty, spindly plants, with few ears, which were poorly filled with kernels due to inadequate soil preparation and fertilization. One year I had healthy, strapping plants with a multitude of giant ears, which were poorly filled due to an insufficient number of plants for good pollination. One year, we had a forest of plants, and bushels of wonderful corn, which all came ripe at once; we ate a few ears that week and gave most of it away. For years, my crop would fall over in the wind and rain; I spent untold hours staking individual plants (one feels kind of silly staking corn). In Texas I've had caterpillars literally demolish entire plants, which kept trying to come back with multiple suckers until they looked like giant bunches of crabgrass with miniature corn ears, each ear with its own private tassle attached (yes, I mean tassle — not silk).

71

And then there was the thing that wouldn't die. It happened in Maryland, in 1983. My plants grew flowers, not tassles, and ears so disgusting I shudder to recall them. It was one of the few times I actually called that County Extension Agent you always hear about. "I think my corn cross-pollinated with something from outer space," I said. "Corn smut," she replied.

Never again. To any of the above. Here's a foolproof corn-growing method that optimizes every important factor. It's a little bit of trouble, but, then again, not nearly so much trouble as staking individual corn plants. And not even close to the trouble of working all season for a harvest of cobs that look like someone already ate all the kernels off of.

First, start with good dirt. I mean real good. True, corn will do all right in just fair soil, if given sufficient water and fertilizer, but our goal is perfection. If you're just starting out, and have followed this book's advice, you will *have* ideal dirt. Over time, however, the humus in your soil will gradually get used up. So if your bed isn't new, work lots of humus into the soil.

Corn is wind pollinated. The male "flowers" are the tassles that appear on top of the plants when the plants are nearing mature size. The female "flowers" are the silk that emerges along the trunk a couple of weeks later. An ear will develop from each clump of silk — normally two ears per plant, about a week apart. The silk remains on the ear, right up until the time you harvest. Each strand of silk leads to one kernel, and must be pollinated if that kernel is to develop. If you plant just one row of corn, the wind will normally not blow enough pollen around for all the kernels to develop. Traditional gardening advice is to plant a "block" of corn, such as four rows of four plants each. The problem with this is that you get a lot of corn all at once!

Of course, if there are 12 or more in your family, you're in business. Or you can freeze most of it. But if you've ever picked fresh ears of sweet corn, marched them straight inside to a pot of boiling water, and then sampled the results, I know you're not growing corn in order to freeze it. You *could* give most of it away, but if you're lazy enough to be reading a book about low-work gardening, I imagine you'll want most of the harvest for yourself.

Red okra. Both foliage and flowers are stunning.

Annual flowers add color and fun to the vegetable patch.

Swiss chard. The red variety is as colorful us it is tasty.

Roma tomatoes.
Supposedly for sauce
and paste, but they're even better
fresh.

Purple-top white globe turnips and French
breakfast radishes.

Bush beans. Tired of "green" beans? Try yellow wax.

Summer squash. (This one is a hybrid, resulting from a cross between yellow crookneck and white bush scallop.)

Eggplant. One of many vegetables with attractive blossoms.

Mixed coles (broccoli, young Brussels sprouts, ornamental cabbage).

Despite traditional gardening advice, I plant my corn a row at a time, to extend the harvest and insure that it all doesn't come ripe at once. But not *too* staggered — only about a week apart. That way, the silk in each row will have the benefit of pollination from its own row as well as from the row planted before and row after. This is possible because the tassles open early and linger late. You will want at least three rows total in your patch. Four is better. Allow one foot spacing between plants in all directions. Four rows of four plants each is ideal for a small family, and will just fill one 4 × 4 bed. For larger families, plant two rows of four at a time, instead of just one. Or, if you have longer beds, you can plant your rows lengthwise, if the orientation of the beds accommodates that. Just remember, each row should be oriented east-west, with the first row planted in the northernmost part of the bed. That way, the taller, older plants will not shade out their smaller, younger siblings.

Here's a secret for getting the roots extra deep, to anchor the plants from uprooting in wind and rain. When it's planting time for your climate zone (about the time of the last average frost), cut the bottoms off some 8-ounce styrofoam cups. Sink one of the bottomless cups into the soil at each spot you intend to plant, so that the top edge of the cup is just above the soil line and the interior of the cup is empty. What you have created are wells, about three inches deep, reinforced to keep the dirt from eroding in.

As you plant, stick the pointed end of a pencil (the gardening tool I use most, I think) straight down into the dirt about 2 1/2 inches deep, at the bottom of each cup, right in the middle. Drop a seed into the hole, and tamp it down the full 2 1/2 inches with the pencil's eraser end. Drop one more seed (just in case), and tamp it down too. Then close the hole. If seeds are planted any deeper, or too near the edge of the cup, they may try to come up outside the cup (especially if your pencil hole didn't go straight down).

When all the cups are planted that you intend to plant that week, fill a styrofoam cup with 15–10–10 fertilizer (use a cup with a bottom), and sprinkle it evenly around the entire planting (except for in the cups them-

Bottomless styrofoam cups provide
reinforced wells, in which corn is planted
extra deep.

selves), allowing one cup for every four plants. Work the fertilizer into the
top inch of soil with your fingers. Then sprinkle half a teaspoon of fertilizer
directly into each cup well.

As with all newly planted seed, moisten the soil daily. You can do this by
squirting water from a cleaned-out old dishwashing soap bottle (my second

most valued tool) into each cup until it's about half full. However, in addition to keeping the soil right around the seeds damp, the whole patch should be watered every few days to work the fertilizer down into the soil. When these plants emerge, the roots will already be deep, and they'll suffer if fertilizer doesn't start to come their way soon.

As soon as your first planting sprouts — normally after about one week (early plantings may take longer) — plant your second, following the same procedures. Plant the third and fourth batches as soon as their respective predecessors germinate. Don't wait much longer, or you will have pollination problems later on.

When plants begin to emerge out of the cups and above the soil line, snip off the ones you don't need at their bases. When each planting is about six inches in height above the soil line (i.e., nine inches total height), carefully loosen the cups, slip them up over the plants, and remove them. Fill the holes with good dirt (or gently mash down the surrounding soil). It won't harm the plants. Quite the contrary, it encourages extra root growth. Then put the cups away for next year.

What all of this results in is healthy, sturdy, deeply rooted plants, which won't lack for moisture if the top few inches of soil dry out in summer and won't blow over in heavy winds and rain. Incidentally, if the soil level in your raised bed drops during the course of the growing season, as the dirt settles and organic matter decays, corn is one crop that allows you to simply pour on more good soil until the box is full again.

As an alternative method of getting the roots deep, I have experimented with simply planting the seed deeper. Seed planted at four, or even six, inches' depth will usually sprout. But it takes longer, and, what's worse, germination time varies greatly, which causes pollination problems later. Also, the plants don't seem as healthy after struggling for two to six weeks, winding their way through twigs and stones and dirt clods. And you can't be sure *where* they'll emerge, either.

As each row germinates, plant the next.

Who would guess that this healthy stand of corn was started in
such an unusual fashion?

Incidentally, although 15–10–10 fertilizer is generally considered a lawn fertilizer, corn is a member of the grass family and will thrive on it. The high nitrogen does not degrade ear production at all, and it certainly adds to the vigor and appearance of the plant. Give your plants a second feeding, in the same amount, six weeks after planting. Or, as an alternative, use slow-release lawn fertilizer, just once, at planting — its nitrogen will last for 2 1/2 months.

Four staggered plantings of four plants each will allow you to pick about 30 ears of corn, over the course of about a month, at a pace appropriate for a family of two to four. Nature being what it is, all plants seeded on a given day will not necessarily produce peak ears at exactly the same time, so you may find that if you pick four ears some evening, two come from one row, with one from the next planting and one from the prior one (this is permissible). Do harvest ears right before cooking. Nothing can match the incredible flavor and texture of just-picked sweet corn. Undercook the ears slightly, by dropping them into water that is already boiling, turning off the heat immediately, and removing them within one to two minutes.

So, does that take care of all the evils mentioned up front? Not quite. The way to outfox caterpillars in south Texas is simply not to grow corn during midsummer. (The best corn in San Antonio is planted in March and gone by June.) Or you might try an organic approach like BT, which is a type of bacteria. Oh yes, if you do live in an extreme climate like south Texas (or Hell), make sure you grow a variety recommended for your area.

And what about "the thing that wouldn't die?" The best way to avoid corn smut is crop rotation. Don't plant corn in the same bed year after year. Raised beds full of perfect garden soil are never wasted and will grow equally outstanding tomatoes or peppers when they're not producing perfect corn.

CUCUMBERS

The cucumber has a noble Near East heritage. One of the most refreshing ways to eat it on a warm summer evening is in a Greek salad. On the island of Crete, they fill a bowl with chilled cucumber slices, add a chunk of feta cheese, and top it off with vinaigrette.

In case you've ever wondered, cucumbers are indeed a member of the same family as watermelons. Also cantaloupes, squash, gourds, and pumpkins. Cucumbers will not, however, cross with any of those other species. They *are grown* much the same. They like loose, humus-enriched soil and warm weather. In areas with short growing seasons, pre-start plants indoors 4–6 weeks early (this allows two weeks for hardening).

The best way to grow cucumbers in a small garden is on a trellis. Although that is undoubtedly not what nature envisioned originally, they do wonderfully grown upright. And whereas cucumbers are often curved when grown on the ground, they turn out relatively straight on a trellis (gravity, I suppose). There are also now some limited space "bush cucumbers," which do not really grow on bushes but on short vines.

Plant cukes well after all danger of frost has passed and daytime temperatures are in the 70's. Even though you'll be growing them upright, leave some open space where roots can grow without competition from other plants — it is best to allow 4–6 square feet per plant. Sow two seeds, an inch apart and an inch deep. Work one cup of 5–10–10 into the top inch of soil of your cucumber patch, being careful not to let the fertilizer come in contact with the seeds. Germination takes about a week, on average. Assuming they both come up, remove the seedling you like the least. As the plant grows, train its runners onto the trellis by tying or looping them around the sticks.

Most varieties are monoecious, producing both male and female flowers. Normally, the first blossoms are male, so don't start sterilizing the pickle jars right away. As with other members of the gourd family, every open female blossom on a monoecious plant will need a male open simultaneously in order to set fruit. If bees are inactive, due to damp, cloudy weather (or because you killed them with insecticide), you may have to hand-pollinate, by plucking a male blossom, removing the petals, and daubing pollen onto female flowers.

Some newer varieties are "gynoecious," meaning, theoretically, all the blossoms are female (although, in actuality, most will produce a few male flowers as well). Many, but not all, of the female blossoms on gynoecious plants will set fruit without the help of male companions (let this be a warning to male *homo sapiens* that genetic research can go too far). If you want more fruit to set, you can grow a monoecious variety with it, to provide additional male blooms. Packets of gynoecious seed may include monoecious pollinator seed.

You can expect your first fruit about 60 days after planting. Pick cucumbers before they get too big. They taste better that way, and plants will be more productive. If left too long, they get seedy and bitter inside, yellow on the outside ... and may actually start to resemble small watermelons in size!

Vines will produce all summer in most areas of the country. However, in weather that is significantly colder or hotter than optimum, cucumbers grow slowly, which makes them bitter. You might as well remove the plants when cool fall weather arrives. In the South, also pull them out when extremely hot summer weather shows up, then start over in late summer for fall harvesting.

The pest posing the greatest threat to cucumbers is the cucumber beetle (two varieties — striped or spotted), which chews up the foliage, stunts growth, and frequently transmits bacterial wilt diseases — which can kill plants almost overnight. (See Chapter 4 for general pest advice.) Fortunately, trellis-grown vines are less susceptible to disease, due to improved air circulation and moisture conditions. Some wilting of cucumber vines is common on hot summer days; don't worry about it, as long as they perk up again in the evening.

For a long time, I couldn't get very excited about cucumbers. They *are* easy to grow. And *very* prolific; maybe that's why I seldom grew them — you can eat just so many slices in salads, and it doesn't take many to fill several pickle jars. Pickling is a fair amount of trouble, and I used to think a quality commercial pickle was just as good as a homemade one. Anyway, I gardened for *fresh* taste.

Then, several years ago, my wife fell heir to an out-of-this-world old family recipe for pickles. Since then, we can't grow enough cucumbers or eat enough pickles (we can finish off a jar with sandwiches and a Redskins game). Suddenly, cucumbers are one of our favorite vegetables from the garden.

♦

BREAD & BUTTER PICKLES

6 lbs. thinly sliced, unpeeled cucumbers (4 qts.)
1 lb. small, thinly sliced white onions ($^1/_2$ c.)
2 large cloves garlic, mashed
$^1/_3$ c. salt
2 qts. ice cubes
4 c. sugar
$1^1/_2$ teaspoons turmeric
$1^1/_2$ teaspoons celery seed
3 c. white vinegar   Yield 7 pt.

In large bowl, mix cucumber slices with onion, garlic, and salt. Cover with ice cubes. Let stand 3 hours. Drain. Remove garlic. Combine remaining ingredients in large pot and bring to boil. Add cucumber and onion. Cook on medium heat for five minutes. While cooking, prepare canning jars and lids by washing with soap and extremely hot water. Fill cleaned jars with hot pickles and juice. Cap and turn upside down (this helps insure that all interior surfaces of jars are sterile). After 10 minutes, turn upright and store.

♦

There are many varieties of cucumber to choose from — short and fat, long and skinny, burpless, picklers... Quite honestly, they're all good and, despite what you might expect, almost interchangeable for use in salads or pickles.

EGGPLANT

Eggplant originated in the Orient, at least 1500 years ago. It migrated through the Mideast, and by 500 years ago had become a staple in European cuisine. Many a French gourmet dish owes its character to the "aubergine." Ratatouille is a delicious mixture of cooked eggplant, tomato, onions, and zucchini. And moussaka, an Athenian's eggplant lasagna, is virtually the national dish of Greece!

Eggplant is a member of the nightshade family, the same as tomatoes and peppers. Its habits and preferences are much the same. And it is subject to many of the same diseases, so if you rotate your crops (see pest and disease section), treat all nightshades as one crop.

Plants are started indoors and transplanted two to four weeks after the average last frost date. Allow eight weeks to reach ideal transplant size, plus two weeks for hardening, or ten weeks total. Seeds are planted at a depth of 1/4–1/2 inch and germinate in one to two weeks.

Eggplants do fine in average garden soil. Mix a moderate amount of humus into the soil at transplanting time. Plant seedlings as deep as their original soil level in your styrofoam cups, or perhaps 1/4–1/2 inch deeper. Allow a two-foot diameter space per plant. Work a half cup of 5–10–10 fertilizer into the top inch of soil over the entire patch, keeping it off the plant itself (refertilize with 1/4 cup per plant after eight weeks). Plants will require support when they bear fruit; the small, inexpensive three-ring wire tomato cages sold at nurseries (which are never big enough for tomatoes!) are ideal for eggplants. As with all newly transplanted seedlings, take care not to let the soil dry out while plants are taking root.

The first fruits mature in 75–90 days. Plants are most productive when the fruits are picked small — about half of their eventual, completely mature size. More importantly, smaller fruits taste the best. Older ones tend to be bitter. When they lose their gloss and start to look dull, you'll know they've seen their day and will contribute more to your compost pile than to your dining delight.

GREENS

The most popular greens in America are probably lettuce, spinach, and chard, in that order. All three are attractive, leafy plants that take up relatively little room in the garden. I always grow more than we need, for ornamental effect.

Lettuce is a cool weather plant. The type most commonly bought at supermarkets is Iceberg, or head lettuce, which requires a long, consistently temperate growing season to mature properly. It provides a lot to eat at once. Better adapted to the home garden is leaf lettuce, which grows faster and can be harvested leaf by leaf. It comes in a number of colorful varieties.

Lettuce is normally started indoors, where it is planted at a 1/4–1/2-inch depth, germinates in about a week, and grows to transplant size in one month. Adding two weeks for acclimatizing, sow seed six weeks before you intend to transplant. Lettuce should be transplanted in spring, at the point at which a few more mild frosts are still likely but a hard frost unlikely. In fall, transplant when the most extreme heat is over. Spacing can be anywhere from 4 to 12 inches, depending on how big you plan to let plants grow — i.e., how much harvesting you intend. Plants do fine in average garden loam. Fertilize with a little 15–10–10 after transplanting, and repeat after 4–6 weeks, or use slow-release lawn fertilizer just once.

In exceptionally cool climates, lettuce will grow all summer. In places that don't receive hard frost, it will grow all winter. Lettuce *can* be direct-seeded in the garden, but to take full advantage of the limited length of cool seasons in most places, transplants are better. Lettuce seed will not sprout when temperatures are consistently below 40 or above 80.

You can begin harvesting about a month after transplanting. Always re-move the larger, outer leaves, near the stalk, with scissors, leaving the smaller, interior leaves. If *all* the leaves are removed, plants will not come out again. In the spring, lettuce will produce until the weather gets fairly warm, at which point quality declines and plants go to seed. In fall, plants produce until the first hard frost (i.e., substantially below freezing for quite a few hours), at which point they die.

Another cool weather green is spinach. In fact, it likes cooler tempera-tures than lettuce and will even survive hard frost, although it will sustain some leaf damage. In the South, it will grow all winter, but won't grow during extended cold spells. Even in "middle America," spinach will often survive the winter; It may not grow, but it will hit the ground running in spring. However, spinach grown over winter tends to "bolt," or go to seed, sooner in spring than spring-planted spinach. You'll know your time is running out when leaves start getting "pointy."

Spinach is normally direct-seeded in the garden, because transplanting is said to be difficult. That advice notwithstanding, I have done both successfully. In fact, I prefer transplants, because: they extend the growing season (spinach goes to seed earlier in spring than lettuce); they make it easier to get plants exactly where you want them (not too close, no bare spots); and in the late summer or early fall, you avoid the problem of seed refusing to germinate due to lingering heat. Just be extra careful not to damage or stress the rootballs when using transplants. Spinach is seeded, spaced, fertilized, and harvested just like lettuce, but you might let the soil dry out a little more between waterings while waiting for seeds to sprout. And allow two weeks longer than with lettuce for seedlings to reach transplant size.

Although spinach is traditionally thought of us a cooked dish, my wife and I love it in salads, with Italian or honey mustard dressing, a little chopped onion and boiled egg, bacon bits, croutons, and fresh ground black pepper. It's truly one of my favorite things from the garden. One plant per person should be adequate for a spinach salad every couple of nights. If you're growing it to cook, plant several times that much, since the volume goes down substantially during cooking. As with lettuce, harvest the larger, older, outer leaves, allowing the smaller, younger, inner leaves to continue growing.

For cooked greens, I far prefer Swiss chard, which is something Americans should probably grow more of. It's attractive (especially the red varieties), hardy, and grows in all kinds of weather — cool, warm, hot. I seed directly in the garden, since there's not much reason to get a head start under the grow light. Plant seeds an inch deep and 6–12 inches apart (depending on how much you intend to keep plants cut back). Each "seed" is actually a small shell, with two (or more) true seeds inside, so you'll probably get two plants from each "seed" sown. Fertilize and harvest like lettuce or spinach. *Red* chard is most attractive when leaves are allowed to get big (plants will grow to a height of 12–18 inches), but smaller leaves make for tastier dining.

Chard is a member of the beet family, which is something you will immediately realize when you pull the plant out of the ground at the end of the growing season.

MELONS

Melons are one of the few things that don't lend themselves to growing in raised, intensive beds, because they require space, both for the vines to spread out and (though we tend to overlook it) for root growth. Given good soil and unlimited space, a single watermelon or cantaloupe plant could cover 100 square feet over the course of a season.

There are two alternatives for the backyard gardener. You can grow one of the new limited-space varieties. Sometimes called "bush" melons, they really are not bushes in the same sense as summer bush squash. Like all melons, limited space melons *do* vine, but the runners are shorter. Both cantaloupes and watermelons are now available in limited-space varieties.

Or you can grow melons on a trellis. In which case, make sure it's a sturdy trellis. And, if growing *water*melons, stick to a small-fruited, "icebox" type, so that the melons will not break from their stems while hanging. Actually, icebox melons are the ideal size for most families anyway, although their quality is perhaps not quite as good as that of larger varieties.

Melons are warm-season (almost hot) crops. Plant them a little later than you would tomatoes and peppers, after daytime temperatures are up in the 80's. Planting too early raises the risk of damping off (a fungus, encouraged by cool and damp conditions, that kills tiny, delicate seedlings). Cool weather also prolongs the seedling stage, which makes plants more vulnerable to being bitten off at the stem by bugs.

Melons can be started indoors, 3–4 weeks early, but it's arguable whether it's worth it in all but the coolest climates. Room temperature is less than ideal for melons (especially *water*melons). You shouldn't start hardening until the weather warms up, at which point you *could* be direct-seeding in the garden. By the time plants reach hardening size, they will be ready for rapid growth but on the verge of outgrowing their containers — which means they pretty much stop growing during the hardening process. All plants grow faster in the garden than in pots — especially *indoor* pots. So 3–4 weeks of "prestarted" growth equates to just 1–2 weeks of direct-seeded, in-garden growth.

Melons like lots of humus and slightly sandy soil. Plant two seeds, three inches apart and an inch deep. They should sprout in about a week. One typical plant — two at most — will be enough for one trellis 4–5 feet wide and the same height. Two plants close together will act like one plant, due to root space limitations, but will tend to send out more runners, which is good for covering a trellis. After planting, work a half cup of 5–10–10 into the top inch of soil (but don't get it directly on the seed) out to a one-foot radius from the plant. Allow at least 8 square feet per plant.

Refertilize, using an entire cup of 5–10–10 over the entire designated melon root growth area, after six weeks. As runners grow, tie or loop them onto the trellis, making sure the vine is especially well supported where fruit is forming.

Melons produce both male and female blossoms. You will recognize the female by the tiny fetal fruit behind the flowers. You need both a male and female bloom open simultaneously — and a bee handy — for fruit to "set." With just one plant, that won't always happen and you will probably only get 3–4 fruit per trellis. Which is about all a limited space melon plant can support anyway, due to restricted root growth. If you suspect a bee shortage, you can pluck the petals from a male blossom (leaving the "stamen" intact), and daub the pollen onto the open center ("pistil") of a female blossom.

Give trellis-grown melons some extra support when they reach softball size. A "sling," fashioned from cloth or old pantyhose, is ideal — use it to cradle the entire fruit, or at least its bottom.

Both cantaloupes and watermelons will produce for as long as warm weather lasts. Your first fruit should be ready to pick 75–90 days after seeding. Cantaloupes are ready to harvest when the end away from the stem turns soft and fragrant — or when the fruit slips easily off the stem with slight turning.

Ripeness is a little trickier to judge in the case of *water*melons. When grown on the ground, the underside of a watermelon will be white, later turning cream-colored, and finally yellow. Harvest when the bottom is yellow. When grown on a trellis, however, watermelons *have* no white or yellow sides, so you'll have to rely on the "thump test." Fruit should sound hollow, not solid, when thumped.

If spitting watermelon seeds is not your thing, there are now seedless varieties available. Although they may not have the absolute best quality flesh, they do not develop seeds, or, at most, produce tiny vestigial ones. Ironically, you *grow* seedless watermelons from seed…and must plant a seedy variety along with it for pollination. "Seedless watermelon seed" is the result of a genetic manipulation.

THE MISUNDERSTOOD OKRA

Okra is a vegetable not widely known in the North. An Eastern gardening expert described it, in all seriousness, as "a cross between a pepper and a squash" (a vicious lie). Still, one can hardly blame her. Okra is a true tropical, which does not cotton to cool weather. It thrives in temperatures in the 90's and even over 100!

Northerners mostly don't know how to eat okra, either. If they've had it all, it was probably pickled. Pickled okra looks (and tastes) terrible. The traditional way to prepare it, across the South, is to cut the pods into half-inch cross sections, shake them up in a bag of cornmeal, then fry the segments in hot oil until crispy. It's delightful that way. Okra is also the staple ingredient in gumbo.

Okra plants are very attractive, with large, exotic leaves and large flowers. The flowers and foliage alone justify growing it, in my book. In very hot climates, plants will grow to heights of eight feet, though six feet is the norm over most of the country. The red variety is particularly ornamental; its pods are just as tasty as the more common green variety and, in fact, turn green when cooked.

Don't bother to plant okra until two weeks after tomato transplanting time for your area. Plants won't do much until it gets hot, and prolonging the seedling stage keeps plants susceptible to being eaten by insects longer (a bug can eat both leaves off a newly sprouted seedling, thereby killing it, in an hour). Allow 18 inches in all directions per plant. Plant two seeds per spot, about an inch apart (remove one seedling when six inches high), and an inch deep. 6–12 plants will feed a family of 2–4. Fertilize with a half cup of 5–10–10 per plant, and repeat every six weeks. Or use slow-release lawn fertilizer as a one-time application. Seeds sprout in one to two weeks. If you like, you can soak seeds in water for 24 hours prior to planting, to soften the seed coats; this will speed up germination by two or three days.

The first pods can be picked (actually, snip them off with small pruning clippers) 45 days after planting in hot climates, perhaps a little longer in regions that are just "warm." After plants are mature, you should harvest at least every other day. Pods are most tender and delicious when just one to two inches long (especially batter-fried!), but it's hard to get enough at once to make a meal. Three to five inches is the usual compromise. Longer than that, they become woody and seedy. When summer heat begins to wane — around the beginning of September in most parts of the country, perhaps a month later in the deep South — pod quality declines, because pods take longer to mature and get woody along the way; when this happens, you might as well remove your okra plants, even though your tomatoes might still be going great!

Okra plants spread out quite a bit, and tend to shade lower crops that are planted too close. Although 12–24-inch spacing is plenty, plant tops will branch out to 24–36 inches' diameter. If you like, you can selectively prune off limbs to allow sunlight in for other plants. In the deep South, if plants get too tall to pick the pods on top, they can be cut back and will come out again, if you're willing to forgo pod production for the several-week period required to rejuvenate (make sure you leave some leaves on the stump for photosynthesis while the bush is coming back).

Obviously, this crop needs space, as well as heat!

ONIONS, ONIONS

"Onions, onions, la la la, I like onions," go the lyrics of an early sixties song. I concur. I especially like, and take pride in growing, large, round, white, sweet, mild-tasting onions.

Onions can be grown from seed, sets, or transplants. We all know what seeds are. "Sets" are tiny, cured, onion bulblets, which are available from nurseries and seed companies in small mesh bags of about 100 and are relatively inexpensive. Transplants are the most expensive way to go and, I think, the least satisfying. If you order transplants by mail, there is also the problem of keeping them fresh. In the northern and central latitudes of the U.S., I recommend sets, since seeds must be started indoors, which is, in my opinion, more trouble than it is worth. In the South, onions can be direct-seeded in the garden—it's cheaper, easier, and more fun to start with seed there.

In the North, grow a "long day" variety, in the South a "short day" variety. The more common varieties are mostly long day onions, and if in doubt about a particular type offered in a seed catalog, you can assume it's long day. If you live "in between," you're probably better off with Northern type onions (and that's probably what you will find in nurseries), but don't expect them to get quite as big as they would at higher latitudes.

Long day onions are planted in spring and mature in summer. Plant your sets several weeks before the average last frost. Onions like sandy soil, with lots of humus, so prepare your bed accordingly. The easiest way to plant is to level the dirt off two inches shy of the top of your frame. Position the sets at a spacing of 1–4 inches, depending on how much thinning for green onions you plan to do. Then cover the bed with 1 1/2 inches of the same kind of dirt you have underneath. For a four-square-foot planting, sprinkle a half cup of 10–10–10 fertilizer (or make your own, using equal parts 5–10–10 and 15–10–10) and a fourth cup of 0–45–0 rock phosphate (it's great for root crops) over the seed bed. Then add another half inch of dirt to cover the fertilizer. Water as you would any shallow-rooted plant in your garden.

If you like green onions, plant thickly. Eventually, however, you will want about four inches between plants, so if you start out with one-inch spacing, you will have to eat a lot of green onions! And there is only about a

Green onions on a bed of spinach and
lettuce

one-month period during which plants are the right size and mildness for green onions — generally, 45–75 days after planting sets.

In the South, plant your short day onions, from seed, in the early fall, after the hottest weather departs, but while it's still "warm." Prepare your bed as a Yankee would, with fairly sandy soil and lots of humus, but level it off just an inch shy of the top of the bed frame. Almost all your seed should germinate if you do things right, so figure out how many green onions and mature bulbs you want. Then mix your seed in an old spice container with 1/4 cup of 0–45 –0 rock phosphate (for a four-square-foot planting) and sprinkle evenly over your designated onion patch. Cover with 1/4–1/2 inch of soil, the same fertilizer dosage recommended above, then another 1/8–1/4 inch of soil. Pat moderately. Then moisten to a depth of 2–3 inches with a sprinkler or nozzle set on fine mist. Moisten the seedbed daily, preferably in late afternoon.

Plants grown from either sets or seeds will emerge in about one to two weeks. Refertilize monthly, in the same amount as your original application (you can forgo the phosphate). In the North, mulch after hot weather begins to set in.

If you want some bulbs to turn out small, for shish kebab or beef Burgundy, cut the tops back to about two inches' height about a month after the green onion stage (they'll come out again). Do it one more time a month after that. Bulb size is proportional to top growth. Plants grown in this manner can be spaced more closely. Simply crowding plants *without* cutting back will also produce smaller bulbs, but a little too large for shish kebab.

It's time to harvest when the tops die back, which is mid to late summer in the North and late spring in Dixie. (If you leave them in the ground, the bulbs will go mushy, sprout new tops when the next season starts, and then go to seed — onions are "biennials.") Clip the dead tops off 1 1/2–2 inches above the bulb. Trim the roots off entirely, unless you like the look of a little stubble. Wash them gently with the hose, and if some discolored skin bothers you, you can remove a little here and there. Let them dry for a week or two at room temperature in open air. We have some hanging wire mesh baskets in the kitchen that work well. In fact, I put my newly harvested onions in the baskets and just leave them there until they're gone (and they go fast — visitors always ask to take one home). We find that even the Bermuda/ Vidalia type onions, which supposedly do not store well, keep just fine for several months at room temperature in our kitchen baskets.

PEPPERS

All homegrown vegetables taste better than their store-bought counterparts, but the difference was never more noticeable than with peppers. Especially a fat, juicy bell that has been allowed to turn sweet and red. Peppers are fun to grow, because there is such a variety of shapes, colors, and tastes. They come blocky, round, or cylindrical. Green, red, yellow ... and everything in between. "Sweet" or hot, mild or strong.

But they are all grown basically the same way.

Plants should be started indoors. Plant seed at a depth of 1/4 inch. Allow eight weeks to reach transplant size, plus two weeks for hardening, or a total of ten weeks. Germination takes about two weeks.

Peppers are warm-weather plants, and should be transplanted about the same time as tomatoes — when daytime temperatures are in the 70's and nighttime temperatures above 50. They do well in average garden loam, but, as with all vegetables, you should add some humus to the soil before planting.

Bell peppers can be very prolific.

Plant seedlings about a half inch deeper than their soil level in your styrofoam cups. 18-inch spacing is about right for most varieties. Then work a half cup of 5–10–10 into the top inch of soil out to a six-inch radius. Refertilize after two months, applying a third of a cup out to a nine-inch radius. Take care that the soil doesn't dry out for the first week or two, until plants take root.

Large-fruited pepper varieties will require support. The inexpensive little three-hoop "tomato" cages available at nurseries are ideal. Put them over your plants from the start; putting them in later can damage the roots a tad. Anyway, they afford protection from cats and kids while the seedlings are most vulnerable.

Peppers are self-pollinating. You can expect your first mature fruit after about 60–75 days in the garden. Never "yank" the fruit off when harvesting, as you can damage the plant; always snip the stem, with small pruning snippers. All peppers can be harvested at any stage of maturity but are more flavorful when left until maximum size. If left until fully ripe, most will change colors, most commonly from green to red. Hot peppers get even hotter at that point, sweet peppers sweeter (and they all get more nutritious). But they won't keep as long, and plants tend not to be as productive if too many fruit are allowed to completely ripen. For the most pounds of peppers, harvest them when they reach full size, but before they change color. Usually, I allow may last flush of peppers in the fall to vine-ripen.

Peppers are easy to grow and almost trouble-free. Most varieties will produce all season in most parts of the country. Most are sensitive to cold, however, and will generally not set fruit when nighttime temperatures exceed the 50–75-degree range (though there *are* varieties that have been bred to do just that). Unlike their cousin the tomato, most peppers are not sensitive to heat; they will set fruit even in daytime temperatures consistently above 100.

Big, blocky bell peppers are excellent stuffed with ground lamb, rice, and onion, then baked. My wife, Karen and I also like them fresh, cut into chunks, with brie cheese, French bread, and red wine. Sweet cherry peppers are perfect for shish kebab. Jalapeños are good pickled or dried. Cayennes are best dried, in my opinion. Larger peppers do not dry well unless you cut them into strips first, but small hot peppers dry nicely whole, in hanging baskets in our kitchen. Cut up with scissors, they make a fine addition to chili.

Incidentally, the seeds in a small dried pepper are perfectly viable for starting transplants the following year. Just remember that if the pepper was a hybrid, the second generation may not be quite the same.

Want to grow a GIANT pepper bush? It's easy in very hot climates, with long growing seasons. Just plant, provide a large (tomato-size) cage, keep the bush watered and fertilized ... and stand back.

To raise a giant in more temperate climates, grow your plant in a large pot (see container gardening section in Chapter 5) for one season. At the end of the season, bring it indoors and park it by a sunny window. Prune and shape

Sweet cherry peppers

it a little, if you like (I like to prune such plants to one large trunk, with three to four medium size "scaffold" branches, much like a fruit tree). The plant won't thrive over the winter, and probably won't produce fruit, but it will be ready to hit the ground running, come spring. In the spring remove the plant from the container and plant it, rootball and all, just like you would a tree or shrub, in your garden. It will grow to enormous size in the garden.

Keep in mind, however, that large plants produce a lot of fruit — probably more than you can eat. And if you want the fruit to reach maximum size (mainly of relevance in the case of *bell* peppers), you will need to thin the fruit some.

POTATOES

Few gardeners grow their own potatoes, figuring a spud's a spud and once it's baked or mashed it doesn't make much difference whether it came from *their* dirt or Safeway's. Others claim homegrown potatoes are fresher and more flavorful, which is true, I think. I'm convinced it's true, anyway, for "new potatoes," which are the young, small ones, dug early in the season. Nor are new potatoes always even available in grocery stores.

I grow my own because it's easy, cheap, and provides some variety in the garden. The foliage is not unattractive. And raised beds are so ideally suited root crops it would be a shame not to grow a few potatoes. That's all I grow, however. "A few." Usually one plant. They laugh at me at the nursery every year when I buy one tiny seed potato, from a bin labeled "$.49 A POUND."

You *can* start with a store-bought root, but why bother when you can buy certified disease-free seed potatoes for a few cents? Supermarket potatoes are not always ready to sprout, since potatoes usually must "age" a little before they will send out shoots. Moreover, grocery store roots are usually treated with a preservative, so that they *won't* sprout. If you start with a store-bought potato, make sure it's one you've had a while and is already beginning to sprout. Otherwise it will probably take so long to sprout in the soil that your crop will be delayed. If you even get one. Most of the time you won't, because the flesh rots before it sprouts.

Potatoes do best in cool to temperate weather. It takes at least 90 days to get reasonable-size roots, 120 for larger ones. If you have a temperate growing

A raised bed is the ideal environment for potatoes. The plant's foliage is an attractive addition to the garden.

season that lasts longer than that, potatoes will get enormous if left in the ground. In warm areas, potatoes will not do much in summer and should be grown as spring or fall crops. Spring-summer potatoes are planted about a month before the expected last frost. If you get frost after sprouting occurs and the top dies back, the plant should grow out again.

For each plant desired, sow one chunk of potato, about 1 1/2" × 1 1/2", with at least one "eye." Or use a small, whole potato. The latter is preferable, because it's less likely to rot on you. Like other root crops, potatoes do best in loose, somewhat sandy soil with a moderate amount of humus. Bury the eyes 4–5 inches deep and 12 inches apart. Space them wider if you're after especially large roots, but only if you have a long enough growing season to *produce* large roots. Sprinkle 1/4 cup of 5–10–10 and 1/8 cup of 0–45–0 rock phosphate over a one-foot-diameter circle above each "seed" and work it into the soil slightly. Then forget about your potato crop for a month or so, other than to insure that the soil doesn't dry out. Sprouting takes 2–4 weeks, depending on the weather.

Each eye you plant will send up a shoot, and the potatoes form on side roots growing off that shoot. If you plant a whole, small potato, expect several shoots. Plants will grow to 18–24 inches in height, with a comparable diameter. New potatoes can be dug any time after the plant flowers, and if you're careful, you can even rob a few new potatoes while leaving the rest to get bigger. Refertilize about the middle of your growing season, and harvest all remaining roots as soon as the plant tops die back.

Here's a trick to increase the harvest somewhat, if your beds are deep enough. After preparing the soil, dig a hole six inches deep and and about the same in diameter. Cut the bottom off an old plastic pot from the nursery and use it to reinforce the hole. Plant your eye three inches beneath the bottom of this reinforced well. Sprinkle a tablespoon of 5–10–10 in the pot. When sprouts begin to emerge, remove the pot and fill in the well with good soil

''Well'' for planting potatoes extra deep

and humus. Now apply fertilizer and rock phosphate as described earlier. By this point, shoots will be growing vigorously and will grow through the added dirt in no time. This method increases the length of the shoots and, therefore, the number of potatoes. (But don't expect the increase to be overwhelming. In fact, I was a little disappointed the first time I tried the technique. I had thought production might double.)

SQUASH AND PUMPKINS

Squash and pumpkins are members of the gourd family. So are gourds, of course. There is a truly amazing variety within this family — shape, color, size... Some varieties (like Turk's Turban) are so bizarre they remind you of something from the "Outer Limits." Within the gourd family, most squash, pumpkin and gourd varieties are categorized into several main species, but each species includes a mixture of things commonly referred to as "squash," "pumpkins" or "gourds." A great deal of crossing occurs within the gourd family, although not all species will cross with all others. A squash plant pollinated by an ornamental gourd will produce normal looking squash, but the seed will be hybrid, and if it's a *summer* squash, which is eaten seeds and all, it may not be as tasty.

Pumpkins do not really lend themselves to backyard gardening, but I grow them occasionally anyway. On a trellis! I like the "Small Sugar" variety for this purpose, since the fruit is relatively small but the flesh is perhaps the finest eating of all pumpkins. There is now a tiny pumpkin called Jack Be Little, with softball-size fruit that can be eaten like squash (although it would take a lot to make a pie!). There are also some so-called "bush pumpkins," which do not really grow on bushes but on short vines, each runner producing just two or three medium-size fruit. Most pumpkin varieties are VIGOR-

Small sugar pumpkin growing on a trellis (supported by a cloth strip)

OUS growers. Vines can quickly consume an entire back yard when grown in-ground!

It's been argued that squash isn't well adapted to limited-space gardening either. There I disagree. I allow a 2 × 2 foot square for each bush type squash plant, though healthy plants will eventually sprawl out of the space and encroach into other plants' territories. You can let them do that, or you can prune them some, or you can site them so they extend over the edge of your bed a little rather than shading out your Swiss chard. I often devote an entire bed to squash and/or pumpkins, planting the seeds near the edge of the bed and leaving the middle open (it doesn't stay open for long). Ideally, every squash plant worth its salt would probably *prefer* a *3 × 3* square, but who's in charge here anyway?

One year I tried growing bush squash in small, hoop-type tomato cages, to confine their sprawling; it didn't work: the weight of the leaves caused the branches to bend down over the wire and break. Staking works better. Nail a stick (vertically, of course) onto your raised bed frame, keep the plant pruned to one main stem, and tie it to the stake with old pantyhose.

Most *vining* squash and pumpkins should be trellised, allowing 6–12 square feet of open space per plant where they won't have to compete for root growth. Shorter-vined varieties can do with less.

One drawback to trellising squash and pumpkins is greater susceptibility to squash borers, which are moth larvae that tunnel into stems and hollow them out, leaving a sawdust-like pulp. When grown in-ground, vining gourds continually put down new roots as they spread; if the borers chew one stem off, there are other stems to keep the plant alive. Not so on a trellis.

The most effective method I've found (and it's far from 100% effective) to rid a squash plant of a borer is to carefully slit open the damaged part of the stem with a sharp knife, inflicting as little additional damage to the plant as possible, and remove the critter with tweezers. Place him on the ground, and position the sole of your shoe on top of him, applying moderate pressure. There is normally only one borer per plant at a time, although that one guy can effect a frustrating amount of destruction. You'll recognize him when you see him as a white caterpillar about an inch long and quarter inch wide. If the infestation is near the ground, mound up dirt around the damaged stem, and it will usually reroot if the damage hasn't progressed too far.

If borer infestation gets out of control on a trellised plant, you can also inject BT (a bacteria that kills caterpillars) or chemical insecticide, using a garden syringe or (if you can get one) large caliber hypodermic needle. The trick is to find the hollowed out spots, which will accept the injection; solid tissue won't take it well.

The most popular bush squashes are yellow ("straight" or traditional "crookneck"), zucchini, and scallop. All three are considered "summer" squash, which means they do not store well and should be eaten fresh. Each summer squash fruit develops in a few days. There are now some limited-space bush varieties, bred especially for home gardeners. These plants are not always as productive, vigorous, or disease-resistant as larger varieties. Nor is the fruit always as good.

The most popular vining squashes are butternut, acorn, and Hubbard; the latter grows enormous fruit and is *definitely* not for limited-space gardens. All three are considered "winter" squash, since they can be stored all winter, under the right conditions (cool and dry). All have hard shells, and each fruit develops over a period of weeks or months. As with bush squashes, there are some vining varieties bred for limited-space gardens. I've found Early Butternut Hybrid, available from Park, to be quite good; each plant sends out one six-foot runner, with four to six fruit, weighing one to two pounds each.

There are also some *winter bush* squash, developed for home gardeners. These include bush acorn and Buttercup, both of which grow on true bush-type plants.

Squash and pumpkins like fairly warm weather, though they can be planted somewhat earlier than tomatoes and peppers. Around the average last frost date is good. They like soil with lots of humus. Seed should be planted at a one-inch depth. Plant two, about two inches apart, then later remove one if they both come up. Work a half cup of 5–10–10 into the top inch of soil around each plant. Germination takes about a week. Bush squash will start producing 45–60 days after planting and will continue until the end of the season or until the squash borers get them, whichever comes first. Usually, the borers get there first; in reality, the average summer squash plant in America probably produces for about a month (see section in Chapter 4 on insects and diseases). Pumpkins and winter squash mature 90–120 days after planting; they are normally harvested all at once, when vines die back in the fall.

Almost all members of the gourd family are "monoecious," producing both male and female flowers. The female blossoms each have a tiny immature fruit attached to the flower. In order for fruit to set, a male flower must be open simultaneously. If you grow only one squash plant, this will not always

If necessary, pollen can be transferred artificially from male to female blossoms, using a cotton swab.

happen and you will, therefore, get fewer fruit. Two plants should be enough to insure that most fruit sets. And they needn't be the same variety to achieve pollination (in fact, mine usually aren't). Yellow squash, zucchini, bush scallops, butternut, acorn, and most pumpkins will cross-pollinate. If you're short on bees (or, regrettably, if you accidentally kill them off through careless use of insecticides), you can artificially transfer pollen from male to female blossoms by using a cotton swab.

Squash and pumpkins can be harvested at any stage of maturity. But summer squash tastes better if picked at the small to mid-size stage (larger fruit are seedy). Winter squash won't taste as good or keep as well if picked early. Young summer squash is great when sliced and steamed (not boiled), then seasoned with butter and fresh ground black pepper.

SWEET POTATOES

They say sweet potatoes thrive in hot, dry, sandy soil. That's not hard to arrange in the Southwest, particularly in a raised bed, where the gardener can control the soil mix. This is a crop that will grow fairly well in "Middle America" (all but the coldest climates), but if you live in a hot climate, you're crazy not to grow some.

I first grew sweet potatoes in south Texas. Knowing absolutely nothing about the subject (except that I didn't want to pay a seed company $12.95 for 25 plants), I simply pulled an old root out of the refrigerator and started a "houseplant," the way country folks have done for generations, by half submerging the root in an old pickle jar full of water, using toothpicks to keep the potato from falling all the way in. It worked when I was a kid. Well, times have changed, and store-bought sweet potatoes are now treated so as not to sprout. By the time my plant rooted and leafed out enough to provide cuttings for transplants, the old potato was decidedly nasty and rotten.

I did get some "slips," nonetheless. I planted two shoots in a 2 × 4 foot patch of a 12-inch-deep raised bed. And did they ever take off! Within six weeks, healthy, strapping vines, which made my houseplant pale by comparison, covered the bed. Subsequently, I had to lop off a foot of growth in every direction weekly to keep the plants from taking over my yard. Though I was beginning to suspect that sweet potatoes were not well adapted to limited-space gardens, I kept at it. In the fall, I removed the vines, just to plant something else, thinking that I might actually find a potato or two. To my utter amazement, I dug up more than a dozen huge, beautiful roots — from that little 2 × 4 foot patch! And I know now that I could have had more had I planted more slips in that space.

I also know now that it's not hard to start your slips from a grocery store root. Pick a fresh one, not one that's been in the crisper a month and is halfway to the rotting stage. A small one is ideal. Wash it thoroughly, to remove as much preservative as possible, gently rubbing with your hands (a scrub brush will damage the skin and eyes) and a little baking soda. Then, *plant* it, like a seed potato (which it is), in a 10–12-inch pot full of potting soil, with the top of the root a couple of inches beneath the soil surface. Keep it indoors, and keep it watered. It should start sprouting in about a month. Then, put it by a window or under a grow light and fertilize with a little 15–10–10. A moderate amount of light is adequate. You might as well enjoy an at-

The author's first harvest

tractive houseplant for several months while waiting for the weather to warm outside.

About tomato planting time for your area, snip off some healthy, six-inch cuttings. Remove the lower leaves and root them in a glass of water for two weeks. During this time, keep the "slips" outdoors, in an appropriate "acclimatizing" location, so that the leaves will harden while the stem roots. Bring them in on cool nights. Then plant the rooted cuttings, up to the top two or three leaves, 12–18 inches apart, in the garden. Because sweet potatoes like hot, not temperate, weather, they should be planted about two weeks after tomatoes go in. Sprinkle 5–10–10 fertilizer and 0–45–0 rock phosphate over the entire patch, using about half a cup of fertilizer and one fifth cup of phosphorous for each plant. Water as you would anything else in your garden.

A fairly sandy soil mix — say two parts sand, two parts topsoil, and one part humus — is ideal. Sweet potatoes can also be grown in large containers. You

Sweet potato ''houseplant''

will have to trim the vines regularly, and refertilize about halfway through the growing season (being careful not to burn the foliage), to insure blocky, desirably shaped roots, rather than long, skinny ones. Sweet potatoes require about four months of warm weather to reach normal size, although they are equally delicious when smaller, and roots will continue to get bigger if left longer in hot climates. When you harvest, remove the roots gently, with your hands, as a shovel or pitchfork can damage the soft tissue.

Sweet potato vines are vigorous growers and must be trimmed back regularly.

Roots will store all winter in a location that is consistently dry and 50–60 degrees (air in the refrigerator is too moist). But that can be hard to find in some parts of the country. If you don't have such a spot, dry the roots for a week at room temperature or lower, then put them in the refrigerator crisper, where they will keep for a month or two.

I finally broke down and ordered some "vineless" or "bunch" sweet potato plants from a seed catalog, in order to obtain stock that would grow less vigorously in a limited-space garden. I thought their produce might also taste better, since presumably they have been bred for fresh taste rather than for surviving long truck rides around the country. True, I didn't need all 12 plants, but it was a one-time investment. Honestly, I can't detect much difference between the seed company's plants and the ones I start from supermarket roots. The produce is all sweet, nutty, and delicious. And the vines will all take over your yard if you don't keep them trimmed back!

Either way, after you've grown sweet potatoes once, you can save a root each fall to start your next "houseplant." As a minimum, that avoids the "preservative problem." To insure that you have a root that keeps that long, don't dig the potatoes until cool weather arrives and the vines start declining, and start your houseplant early.

TOMATOES – EVERYBODY'S FAVORITE

Without question, the most popular vegetable grown in gardens across America is the tomato. And no wonder. Few vegetables can match the taste of a sun-grown, vine-ripened tomato, fresh from the garden. Perhaps the purest way to appreciate it is to slice it, drizzle it with olive oil, and sprinkle on some fresh, chopped basil. And probably no other vegetable (yes, I know the tomato is technically a fruit, not a vegetable) generates as much pride as a large, perfectly round, blood-red, blemish-free tomato.

PLANTING ADVICE

Tomatoes like full sun and warm weather. The ideal climate would have daytime temperatures in the mid-eighties, with nighttime temperatures in the mid-sixties. There is no point in transplanting tomatoes until spring temperatures have generally warmed up to 70-degree days and 50-degree nights. Plants won't grow much while it's still cooler than that (they certainly won't set fruit) and will not fight off insects and diseases well. A mild frost of several hours' duration will kill a tomato plant.

Tomatoes also like deep, loose soil, rich in humus. Before planting, work a generous amount of compost, or fine bark mulch and peat moss, deep into the dirt. I normally allow about a 2 × 2-foot square for each tomato plant. If you support your tomato on a stake or trellis nailed to your wooden bed frame, you will obviously plant near the edge of the bed, but still allow an appropriate open space where the roots can grow without having to compete with other plants.

Tomatoes should be started indoors, eight weeks before the desired transplant date (this allows two weeks for acclimatizing). Plant seed at a half-inch depth. Germination normally takes one week.

When transplanting, pluck the lower leaves off each seedling. Gently remove the root ball from the cup and, cradling it carefully in your hands, bury the root ball and stem up to the few leaves remaining on top. Buried stem portions will grow extra roots, making for healthy, deeply rooted plants. If a seedling is "leggy," due to insufficient light, and thus too tall to bury upright in your raised bed, you can bury it at an angle, or bury it horizontally, bending the top few inches up through the soil surface; the exposed stem portion will soon straighten up and be growing erect.

Next, work a half cup of 5–10–10 fertilizer into the top inch of soil covering the entire patch you have designated for each plant, being careful not to get it on the plant itself. Repeat with half that much fertilizer every six weeks thereafter.

PROBLEMS

Under no circumstances should you use high-nitrogen fertilizer, such as 15–10–10. Heavy nitrogen does make for lush, green, leafy growth — but no tomatoes!

Other problems encountered by tomato growers can be blamed on inconsistent watering. One such outcome is cracking, or splitting, of fruit, which happens when plants that have become accustomed to a slow, steady supply of water — or are just barely surviving on a ration that is really not quite sufficient for healthy growth—suddenly receive an abundance of the stuff for two or three days. Another water-related frustration is blossom end rot, identifiable by a black, rotten, spongy spot on the bottom of the tomato (where the blossom originally was). Its direct cause is calcium deficiency, which, in turn, is caused by irregular watering.

Heat can be problematic. Too *little* warmth will keep portions of green fruit from turning red. Fruit exposed to too *much* sun or heat will suffer from "sunscald," a condition in which portions of fruit turn yellow and soft. Temperatures above 90 or below 50 will usually cause blossoms to drop off before setting fruit. Spritzing with tomato "blossom set" spray, available at nurseries, will normally correct that, though too much spritzing causes malformed fruit. A little extra phosphorous in the soil at planting time works almost as well.

One *good* thing about tomatoes: the blossoms are self-pollinating. Well, almost. You still need a bee, or wind, to stir things up *within* each flower. But, in any case, you need not grow more than one plant for the sole reason of insuring good pollination.

TYPES

Horticulturists classify tomatoes as "determinate" or "indeterminate." The former group, theoretically, consists of plants that grow to a certain size and then stop, while the latter grow indefinitely. In reality, however, the difference is not clear-cut. In cool climates, most tomato varieties, determinate or in, grow all seasons and die in the fall. In hot climates, most tomatoes, determinate or not, grow all spring and begin dying when 95-degree weather hits. A "bush" tomato is a determinate that is especially compact and ripens most of its fruit concurrently, which is perfect for commercial harvests.

Non-bush determinates (sometimes called "vigorous determinates"), and all indeterminates, ripen a few fruit at a time over an extended period. Most seed on the market is identified as indeterminate. But I wouldn't pay too much attention either way.

One thing I *would* pay attention to is disease-resistance. Capital letters after the variety name indicate the combination of disease resistance for which the plant has been bred. The most common are V (resistant to verticillium wilt), F (fusarium wilt), N (nematodes), and T (tobacco mosaic). Every year there seem to be more. And while I've never been particularly plagued by such diseases, it might be because I normally *grow* tomatoes that *are* at least "VF" if not "VFN" or more. Regardless, there are so many disease-resistant tomato varieties available today that, all else being equal, there is no reason to settle on one that's not.

Seed companies, as opposed to horticulturists, categorize tomato varieties based on such factors as size of fruit and how long they take to ripen. The "dividing lines" between groups are somewhat fluid and arbitrary. And categories are not mutually exclusive.

When we say that a given variety requires 70 days to mature, we mean from transplanting, not seeding. And we mean that that's how long it takes for the *first* fruit to ripen — not all of them. Be advised that the advertised "days to maturity" is a very rough approximation only. Different seed catalogs don't always agree. Much depends on your climate and, especially, the weather in a given year. Also, seed producers tend to exaggerate how fast their varieties mature.

The "main season" tomato group includes most of the more commonly grown varieties ... and also most of the more versatile varieties, in terms of disease resistance and adaptability to different climatic conditions. Most main-season tomatoes mature around 70–75 days from transplanting, and produce fruit that is high-quality and medium-to-large in size.

Most "early" varieties mature in about 60–65 days. They're ideal for cool climates, with short growing seasons. Ironically, they also provide one of several ways to deal with extremely *hot* climates, in which tomato growing can only be successfully accomplished during brief spring and fall seasons. And for all of us, of course, early varieties make it possible to start harvesting some tomatoes early in the season.

Early varieties supposedly have been bred to withstand cold better than others and ripen fruit at a faster rate. Actually, my own experience is that (1) there's not much difference in cold (or heat) tolerance and (2) early fruit ripen faster mainly for the simple reason that they're smaller and therefore don't take as long to grow. Fruit from most early varieties fall in the small-to-mid-sized range. Generally, their quality is not quite as good as that of later-maturing varieties, but a vine-ripe tomato is a vine-ripe tomato, especially when you haven't had one in eight or nine months.

"Late-season" varieties take 75–85 days to mature. There is no particular advantage to waiting that long. The quality is not necessarily better (and sometimes worse). It's just that some varieties *take* that long, and if you want to grow one of those varieties, that's how long you'll have to wait. This category includes many heirloom, canning, and paste tomatoes — all of which are often considered categories in themselves.

Late-season varieties also include "beefsteaks," the giant, "bragging" tomatoes you always see pictures of. They too comprise a category in their own right. Beefsteaks reach a size of 1–3 pounds apiece, but suffer in quality. They tend to have relatively more hard white membrane inside, rather than consistent red flesh. They also tend to be lumpy and misshapen on the outside. In short, they've been bred with one purpose in mind, and one purpose only — picture-taking.

At the other extreme are cherry tomatoes, the one-inch or marble-size fruit so good for salads and snacking. Most grow on full-size plants. And they're often so prolific that you'll have a hard time keeping up with them.

"Standard" tomatoes are basically for commercial growers and have nothing in particular to recommend them to backyard gardeners. A typical standard tomato would be a non-hybrid bush determinate, not particularly disease-resistant, producing medium-size fruit, which all ripen about the same time. Some standard fruit are relatively low in water content and, therefore, ideal for canning. Others excel at ripening in boxes, after being harvested green.

Some varieties produce small plants, which are well adapted to container-growing. "Patio" tomatoes do well in 12–18-inch diameter pots, with a comparable depth; most produce fruit that are plum-size — larger than cherries but smaller than "earlies." "Basket" tomatoes do fine in 6–8-inch pots — and produce a few cherry tomatoes each.

Both patio and basket plants can also be grown in the garden, where they will get a little bigger and produce slightly larger fruit. Most veteran gardeners don't consider their quality sufficient to warrant tying up garden space on them, but a vigorous, compact patio tomato plant can be much more attractive than a sprawling, unkempt-looking large variety, so I sometimes grow them in the garden, as much for looks as taste (that's allowed). Anyway, ALL homegrown tomatoes are delicious.

Other tomatoes are essentially novelties — yellow tomatoes, white ones, pink, low-acid, long-keepers, stuffers… You may want to try one now and then, for fun, but you probably won't come to rely on them as your staples.

I won't make any recommendations as to particular varieties. Too much depends on your personal likes and the conditions where you garden. Also, new varieties are continually being developed and tested, so any advice we gave here would have to be modified annually. Anyway, tomato varieties are surprisingly interchangeable with regard to how they are used. They can all be made into delicious pizza sauce, for example, while Roma paste tomatoes are one of my personal favorites for eating fresh. And homegrown, vine-ripe tomatoes of even the worst quality are still outstanding compared to those terrible pink things the supermarkets sell in January.

MEANS OF SUPPORT

Almost all tomato plants — even bush varieties that are advertised to the contrary — require support. If you choose to stake them, nail a six foot 1 × 1 inch stick onto your raised bed, and plant by the stake, near the edge of the bed (the roots will grow out into the middle of the bed). You will have to keep the plant pruned back to one main stem, because that's all a single stake can support. That means that about once a week you will have to snip off some branches, some of which may have blossoms and perhaps even tiny fruit. It's a painful process (for the gardener), but must be done. Tie the stem to the stake every foot or so, with thick string or cloth strips, being careful not to cut into plant tissue. Some side branches will be determinate and will stop growing after 9–18 inches; leave them. Others, called "suckers," are indeterminate branches, which emerge from the crotches between the main stem and older, determinate side branches; snip them off.

If you prefer a trellis, nail two vertical 1 × 1 stakes onto the bed, two feet apart, with horizontal 1 × 1's nailed to the vertical sticks at one-foot intervals. How tall and how wide the trellis should be depends on the length of your growing season and how much space you are allowing for the roots to grow (plants with a lot of root space grow bigger). A good average size trellis, though, would be about four or five feet high and about the same width. You needn't prune much if you use a trellis. Simply train and tie branches onto the trellis.

The *easiest* support to provide is a cage, because you don't have to do any tying *or* pruning — you just let the plant go, occasionally tucking a wayward branch back into the cage.

You can make a cylindrical cage out of concrete reinforcing mesh. Two-foot diameter and five-foot height is about right. Cut some horizontal strands off the bottom, leaving vertical wire "stakes" you can push into the soil for anchoring. Make sure the mesh is large enough to reach your hand in and pull out the size tomatoes you intend to grow! One problem with con-

Staked tomato plant

crete reinforcing wire is that you usually have to buy a 50-foot roll, out of which you might use half, but if you can go halves with another gardener, you're in.

You can also buy ready-made tomato cages, but most are too small (I don't even know why they make those little three-hoop jobs you see in all the nurseries every spring!) and plants quickly outgrow them. One seed company sells rectangular cages, which are a little small (and a little expensive), but can be combined to form bigger ones.

119

Tomato in a cage

With all caged plants, regardless of cage size, some branches, heavily loaded with fruit, will hang down over the wires. Contrary to what you might expect, however, this won't break the branches or cut off circulation. It just looks funny.

THE BIG, THE MOST, AND THE EARLY

In general, cages are probably the best way to go. Not only are cages the least trouble, but caged plants consistently produce the most pounds of tomatoes — and the prettiest ones, since the concentrated foliage protects the fruit from sunscald.

Staked plants produce the largest, albeit fewest, fruit. If you want to grow the biggest tomatoes possible, choose a beefsteak variety, stake it, and prune each cluster of tomatoes down to one fruit. You'll only get about five or six tomatoes off the whole plant, and they won't be the absolute finest quality, but they'll be enormous.

The way to get the *earliest* tomatoes is to grow a fast-maturing patio variety, in a large pot. Set it out in the spring, several weeks before you are ready to transplant main-season tomatoes into the garden. Bring it in every night and on cold days until genuine summer weather arrives.

Fortunately, you don't have to choose between the most, the biggest, and the earliest. You can grow one early patio plant in a pot, one main-season plant in a cage, and one staked-and-pruned beefsteak. Then you can have the best of all worlds.

EASY PRESERVATION TECHNIQUES

There are bound to be times when you'll have too many ripe tomatoes to eat at once. You can give some to the neighbors. Take some to work. Such generosity is one of the rewarding traditions of the gardening fraternity. You can also simply throw them in a bag in the freezer, closing the top with a twist-tie, for use later in soup or sauce. If you anticipate them being there longer than 2–3 months, *double*-bag them, for added protection from freezer burn.

When you're ready to make spaghetti sauce or stewed tomatoes (we use the latter in chili con queso), drop the frozen tomatoes, a couple at a time, into a pot of boiling water. Remove them after a few seconds, and the skins will slip right off, while the "bodies" remain frozen (you may have to apply a sharp knife point around the stem if any hard "core" is attached to it). Put the frozen, peeled tomatoes into a crockpot, adding whatever spices you like, turn the heat on high, and leave the lid off. You won't need to add water.

This is one of the easiest, least messy ways to cook sauce. It's one of the easiest way to store an overabundance of fresh tomatoes. And it insures that you have *enough* fresh tomatoes at once to *make* a pot of sauce, which won't otherwise always happen if you grow only one plant.

ALL GOOD THINGS . . .

One of the saddest moments in life for a gardener is that autumn evening when the first frost hits.One day your tomato plant is healthy and productive and enjoying life to the fullest. The next day it's as dead and limp as old weeds in a vacant lot. You can't change that. But you can salvage something out of the disaster. When the first frost is predicted, go ahead and pick all the tomatoes that are partly red or have turned from light green to dark green. You can ripen them indoors. Tomatoes that are still *light* green will not ripen indoors, but they can be sliced and fried (surprisingly good — much like egg-plant) or sliced and pickled (not delicious, in my opinion); small ones can be pickled whole.

When ripening green tomatoes indoors, common advice is to "do it in the dark." My personal experience is that green tomatoes ripen equally well in the dark, the shade, indirect light, or even that much feared "sunny window sill" that the experts warn us to avoid.

Here are some other things the "experts" recommend. Repot seedlings several times, during "pre-season," using progressively larger pots. Cut back watering and fertilizing a week before you start hardening transplants. Start your hardening with just two hours of sun a day, gradually working up to full sun. Do your transplanting on a cloudy day. Deliberately amputate some roots (i.e., "root-prune") from healthy, growing plants, to encourage early fruit ripening. Do not harvest within two days of a full moon (okay, I admit it, I made that one up). Remove small green tomatoes late in the season, since they won't have time to ripen and will draw energy from fruit that *does* ripen. Don't smoke near your tomato plants, because the plants will catch tobacco mosaic. HAVE THEY LOST THEIR MINDS? Or do they just like to make things more difficult?

In the final analysis, growing tomatoes is really not all that complicated. If it were, the average American couldn't do it. And as the author of a gardening book, my goal should be to make the process simpler, not harder. Anyway, one of my favorite things in life is smoking my pipe while playing in the garden.

TURNIPS AND RADISHES

Like most root crops, turnips and radishes are cool-weather vegetables, grown in spring and fall most places, though they grow all summer in especially cool climates. One type of turnip, the rutabaga, is grown almost exclusively in cool climates, because it takes so long to mature. The most popular turnip nationwide is probably the old standby Purple Top White Globe. "Turnip greens" (the tops), cooked like spinach, are popular among many Southerners. The best greens come from varieties bred specifically for that use, such as Seven Top; these varieties grow very small roots, which aren't particularly tasty or useful.

Both turnips and radishes handle mild frost very well. In most climates, plant them a month or so before the expected last spring frost. Replant in late summer or early fall in time for the majority of root development (the last half of the plant's life) to occur in 50–80-degree temperatures. Turnips and radishes will grow all winter in much of the deep South.

Turnips take 45–60 days to mature (except for rutabagas, which require 90) and should be spaced at 3–6 inches, depending on the variety (allow 10–12 inches for rutabagas). Most radishes mature in 30–45 days; 1 1/2–2-inch spacing is about right for radishes. Since radishes grow so quickly and you can eat only so many at a time, you will probably want several small succession plantings, a week or two apart. You can plant as few as nine at a time, if you like (it's your garden) in little 6 × 6-inch squares.

Both turnips and radishes enjoy loose, slightly sandy soil, and raised beds are perfect. Add some soft, fine compost, and level the soil off one inch below the top edge of your frame. I don't recommend "broadcasting" turnip or radish seeds. It wastes seed, requires thinning, and leaves bare spots. Unlike carrot seed (for which there are several good reasons to broadcast), turnip and radish seeds have a high germination rate and, though small, are big enough to handle easily. Lay down one seed every place you want a plant. Then sprinkle a 1/4–1/2-inch layer of soil over the seeds, rubbing the dirt between the palms of your hands to keep it fine and even. Don't use pure topsoil, as it tends to crust and hamper germination. Sprinkle on 5–10–10 fertilizer, at a rate of 1/8 cup per square foot. Add 1/8–1/4 inch more dirt, to hold the fertilizer. Then pat everything down moderately. Finally, mist with a nozzle set on fine spray. Dampen daily until germination, which takes about a week usually.

Turnips and radishes grow partly above ground, so, if you never grew them before, don't be alarmed and start covering them up with more dirt. Do harvest when roots reach the appropriate size. Leaving them in the ground longer makes them woody, as does too much heat.

Radishes are a great way to introduce children to gardening. They're easy to plant. And what other crop can grow up and mature during the attention span of a six-year-old?

Don't Forget To "Add Flower"

Although they're not vegetables (not even technically), there's no rule that says you can't plant some flowers in your vegetable garden. Even if you're not a "flower person" (I'm not), flowers add color and make what might otherwise be a rather utilitarian-looking "farm-in-a-box" eye-pleasing. I started sticking some flowers in when I realized the main reason I gardened was not to feed the family, but for fun.

You can take one of several approaches. You can simply use flowers to fill in vacant corners. A 2 × 2-foot square you've designated for a tomato plant probably won't have much root growth in the corners, since plant roots grow out in all directions at once, thus tending to form circular patterns. Or you may want to reserve strategic spots for flowers when planning your garden, to insure that the flowers add the maximum visual effect. You may even want to reserve an entire 4 × 4-foot bed for flowers. Or let shallow-rooted, creeping flowers surround your deeper-rooted tomatoes and peppers.

You will generally want annuals, not perennials, because the latter would restrict crop rotation and wind up dictating what vegetables you could grow where each year. However, I've grown daisies as annuals by simply removing them at the end of the growing season. Personally, having gardened in a lot of different places, I do opt for flowers that are well adapted to the local area, because I don't want to have to fool with them much. I prefer to spend the majority of my gardening time growing vegetables, not baby-sitting flowers.

Some flowers to consider: daisies (they look old-fashioned and "rural," even if they *are* perennials), marigolds (they are said to keep insects away, though *I* haven't found them to be particularly effective at it), impatiens (they'll grow in partly shady spots), coleus (adds a variety of color and also does well in shade), giant sunflowers (give them room, like corn or okra), and gazanias (they do great in hot, dry climates).

With some caution, I add my vegetable garden flower of choice, portulaca, to the list. Once you grow it, it will keep coming back from seed (thousands of tiny plants!) in your garden each spring, like weeds. Every time I see another 20 or 30 sprouting, I'm reminded of the words Boris Karloff haunts Toddy with in *The Body Snatcher*: "You'll never get rid of me, never get rid of me…" They're "nice weeds," though. I never have to reseed, they're shallow-rooted (and, thus, take little away from my vegetable plants), and it's easy to kill the plants, if you want to, when you work the soil. Best of all, wherever bare spots occur in my garden, the portulaca fills in, providing a natural-looking landscaping unity.

You can order your flower seeds the same time you order vegetable seed, since most catalogs offer both. The ones that need a head start can be started indoors the same time you start your tomatoes and peppers. Fertilize with 5–10–10, to keep them healthy and encourage blossoms.

FOLLOWING THROUGH

MAINTAINING HEALTHY SOIL

If your garden is new, and you set it up the way this book recommends, your soil will be a loose, friable, perfectly proportioned blend of topsoil, humus, and sand. If you plant according to this book's recommendations, your soil will have the perfect combination of nitrogen, phosphorous, and potassium, the three main plant nutrients. In short, you will have perfect soil.

Maybe. There is a chance you could be missing an important trace mineral or two, particularly if you started out with all store-bought ingredients. Trace minerals include iron, calcium, magnesium, manganese, sulfur, and several others. Plants don't need much of these, but they do need a little. A deficiency could show up in stunted plant growth, misshappen or chlorotic (yellowed) leaves, small fruit, tomato blossom end rot ... or oddball, otherwise inexplicable problems (one newly established bed of mine grew bell peppers that ripened and turned red at one inch in diameter!). Just to be safe, you may want to add a trace mineral supplement to your soil the first year. After the first year, trace mineral deficiencies are seldom a problem (and they *may* not be the first year), because your garden will obtain these elements from various combinations of organic matter that you dig into your soil.

You should add humus to your soil every time you plant something, because old humus "goes away" by getting converted to soil. The main benefit of humus is that it increases moisture retention, but a side benefit is that it adds nutrients. Leaves, grass clippings, bark mulch, peat moss, compost ... they all contribute. Tree leaves are an especially good source of trace minerals, because tree roots go down deep and bring up some strange substances from the rocky substrata. Kitchen waste is a good source — banana skins, orange peels, eggshells, coffee grounds, tea bags ... think of the strange and wonderful combination of minerals such organic matter must provide. The wider the variety of humus, the better for your soil.

I save everything. We always keep a three-pound coffee can under the sink, and all kitchen waste goes into it. It stinks every time you open it. My wife hates it. But I love it, and if you're a gardener, you will too. I know it's tacky, but I even carry cans of used coffee grounds home from work, paper filters and all. It's great stuff. It all either gets dug directly into the garden or it goes into the compost pile. (Then, the empty cans goes under the sink!)

Any of the above sources of organic matter can be dug directly into your garden soil, during the "off season" (if the soil is workable) or between crops. The simplest method is to scoop out a shovelful of dirt, dump in the organic matter, put the dirt back on top, then forget about it. Move to a new spot each time you dump. This is an especially good way to get rid of fish heads and innards (bury them deep, so they won't smell and attract cats — they take a while to decay!).

During peak gardening season, however, you will not often have a vacant area of garden you can dig in without damaging plant roots. That's when a compost pile is helpful.

A compost pile in an out-of-the-way
corner. The fence here has been varnished
to prevent rot.

The "experts" have recipes for successful composting. One part this, one layer of that. Buy some bone meal to add, some fertilizer. Humbug. I refuse to compost according to a recipe. It's too much like work. And I refuse to *pay* for things to go in my compost pile. The whole idea was to get beneficial garden additives from stuff "normal" people (i.e., non-gardeners) throw away! Basically, all organic waste around our house and yard goes into the compost pile (well…*almost* all), including doggy piles (I know, it's gross, but I have to do *something* with it). There are some limits, however. You don't want too many fresh grass clippings, because they'll turn to slime. You don't want too much ash from the fireplace, because it makes the compost — and eventually your soil — too alkaline. And avoid meat, fat, and grease — they attract animals and don't break down well.

The ideal composition is a fairly balanced mix of green, juicy stuff (e.g., fresh grass clippings); gross, gooey stuff (kitchen waste); dry, soft stuff (dried leaves or dried grass clippings); and more "substantial" stuff (nut shells, sawdust, shredded tree branches, and rotten bark that falls off firewood). Where most people go wrong is too much of the first two categories above, which turns the whole pile into cold, airless muck. A compost pile that's working will be extremely hot in the interior (stick your hand in to find out), from bacterial action.

For best results, turn the pile occasionally with a pitchfork, to aerate it. There is also an English-made tool (leave it to the Brits — great gardeners!), only recently available in the U.S., that you may want to try. It's a rod, with a handle, that you poke down into the pile. When you lift up, the spring-loaded tip expands, pulling the pile apart. It's easier, and less messy, than pitchforking, although the gunkier portions of your pile will clog the tip, requiring cleaning with your fingers every few plunges.

Composting under ideal conditions results in beautiful, moist, crumbly, black soil. But I don't worry much about that. My compost pile is actually just a place to store organic waste until I need some for the garden. I fork it over every month or so, but often the stuff I remove and use is not really very far along the path toward finished compost. That's okay. It's my pile. I must point out, however, that "underdone" compost often contains bugs, insects, or maggots, which may require termination with extreme (chemical) prejudice if added to your garden.

Black gold: perfect compost.

Although humus will normally provide your garden with sufficient trace nutrients, it seldom provides enough of the big three, nitrogen, phosphorous, and potassium. To get these, you will have to make a concerted effort. The obvious way, and, for most us, the cheapest, is commercial fertilizer, often disparagingly referred to as "chemical" fertilizer by organic purists. Actually, there is nothing unnatural about it. It contains the three chemical elements plants in nature need most. And it comes from substances mined from the earth, as well as "organic" sources such as urea.

During most of my gardening career, I have relied exclusively on two fertilizer formulas: 15–10–10 for corn and green, leafy crops; 5–10–10 for the rest, except onions, for which I use half and half (thereby creating 10–10–10). As a general guide, the rate to apply for all the above is about one cup for every 4–8 square feet of soil surface. The precise amount is not critical. However, I don't like to waste fertilizer, so I never fertilize the whole garden.

Instead, I fertilize each crop individually as I plant it. Some fertilizers will burn foliage, so keep it off the plants themselves. Use the cheapest, most generic fertilizer you can buy (potassium is potassium), and buy it in large bags, not little boxes.

Recently, I've begun experimenting with "slow-release" lawn fertilizer, for plants that like a lot of nitrogen and will be in the garden longer than two months — i.e., corn and greens. The nitrogen pellets in slow-release fertilizer are coated with sulfur, in varying, random thicknesses. Approximately half of the nitrogen is released during the first 30 days, the rest over the following 45 days. It is more expensive, but saves refertilizing.

In addition to the above fertilizers, I add a little rock phosphate for root crops, which thrive on phosphorous. If you have a problem with tomato blossom drop, extra phosphorous in the soil will help that too ("blossom set" spray is essentially phosphorous). The general dosage is about one cup of 0–45–0 "triple phosphate" for 16 square feet of garden. Use proportionately more if the rock phosphate is less potent. E.g., "super phosphate" has a 0–30–0 formula, and "ordinary" phosphate 0–15–0, although recent studies suggest the "ordinary" product may not break down fast enough to do as much good as we once thought. Bone meal, although a little expensive, will also provide phosphorous. So will soft, crumbly chicken or fish bones, left-over from boiling for soup. Bones that have not been ground and steamed, or boiled soft, do little, however, except attract cats and dogs.

You can fertilize entirely "organically" if you prefer. (Actually, "organic" is a misnomer in this sense, because not all natural fertilizers originate from living organisms.) It's more fun for some people, just as baking bread is more fun than buying it. The most readily available sources of nitrogen are manure and urea (now *that's* organic). You can usually get both, mixed with straw, free for the asking at a local riding stable. Call and ask first, of course, and take your own plastic trash bags. As already noted, both bone meal and rock phosphate provide phosphorous. And wood ash is high in potassium. There are other, more obscure, sources, including blood meal (nitrogen), fish emulsion (nitrogen and phosphorous), greensand (potassium), and seaweed (potassium), but all are expensive unless you have a friend in the rendering plant or Davy Jones' locker.

It's tricky business using natural fertilizers. Fresh manure is *too* high in nitrogen and can burn foliage ... or make for all foliage but no fruit. It also contains weed seeds, which *do not* make a good addition to your soil. It's advisable to let fresh manure rot awhile first, or add it to your compost pile (compost piles work better with some added nitrogen anyway).

You should check your soil acidity at least once a year, using litmus paper, which is relatively inexpensive and can be ordered from seed catalogs. You definitely should check it when you first establish your raised beds. The measure of alkalinity or acidity is called pH. The scale runs from 0 (extremely acidic) to 14 (extremely alkaline), with 7 being neutral. It's a logarithmic scale, so 6 is 10 times as acidic as 7. 8 is 100 times as alkaline as 6. If soil is too alkaline or acidic, the effect is to "lock up" certain nutrients and make them unavailable to plants. Different vegetable plants do best in different pH ranges, but I can't think of any that will do well outside the 5–8 range. A range of 6 to 6.5 (slightly acidic) will satisfy virtually all, so that's what you should shoot for.

Various factors could cause your pH to get out of whack, even if you start out in the ideal range when you first set up your beds. One such factor is the local water supply. Another is the types of humus you add to your soil. To make soil 1 pH unit lower (more acidic), add one styrofoam cupful of sulfur for 50 square feet of soil surface (e.g., three 4 × 4 beds or two 4 × 6 beds). To raise the pH 1 unit (make it more alkaline), add one cup of lime for 16 square feet of soil.

As previously noted, you can also add wood ash to raise the pH. But go slow. I used to dump all our fireplace ashes into the compost pile. While establishing a new raised bed one year, I used compost for about half of the fill. I checked the pH in the new bed one day, just for the heck of it. It was off the scale! Never before or after in my life have I seen apparently good garden soil that was so alkaline!

One last thing you should do to keep your soil healthy: crop rotation. Farmers have rotated crops for hundreds of years. One reason is that each type of vegetable depletes a different combination of nutrients from the soil, and if you continually grow the same thing in the same spot, you increase the chances of a deficiency. Also, when a crop is done, farmers have traditionally turned it back into the soil — you should do likewise — and since each type of dead vegetable plant *returns* a different combination of nutrients to the soil, rotation encourages a healthy variety of minerals in your soil.

Perhaps the most important reason for rotating crops in the backyard garden, however, is that particular plants are prone to specific viral or bacterial diseases, as well as specific bugs, caterpillars, or insects. Rotation "breaks the cycle." For example, if the soil around your tomatoes contains tomato wilt disease, planting your next tomatoes in a different bed will give them a wilt-free growing environment, while the wilt-contaminated soil will not harm a different kind of plant, like corn. Many pests go through life cycles, such as egg-caterpillar-moth. Rotating crops can deny the critters anything useful to eat during one stage, thus averting future stages.

One critter I do like in my garden is the earthworm, which is the ultimate symbol of healthy soil. Good soil will have lots of worms. Unless you use insecticide regularly. It's sometimes a difficult choice.

PESTILENCE AND DISEASE

All gardens attract pests. However, since this is the least fulfilling aspect of gardening, it has never been my intent to become an expert on identifying different species of bugs and insects (nor am I going to teach you). I'm not a scientist. I'm a gardener. I know what I like in my garden, and I know what I don't like. I try to keep the things I like alive, and I try to use a common sense approach to get rid of the things I don't like.

So, from my common sense, non-scientific perspective, here are the more common pests that inhabit vegetable gardens:

♦ ANTS: More of a menace to gardeners than gardens, especially "fire ants," which are colonizing the South.

♦ APHIDS: Teeny-tiny guys who hatch out of teeny-tiny eggs by the hundreds on the undersides of leaves. They suck juice out of leaves and cause leaf distortion and stunted growth.

♦ BEETLES: There are many different kinds, such as the Japanese beetle, cucumber beetle, June bug (despite the name, it's a beetle, not a true bug), blister beetle, Mexican bean beetle, and Colorado potato beetle. They eat foliage and sometimes fruit.

♦ BUGS: Another diverse group, including the squash bug and stink bug. They suck the juices out of plants, and, if infestation is severe enough, can kill them.

♦ CATERPILLARS: The larvae of moths and butterflies, including:

CABBAGE LOOPER: Feeds not only on the cabbage family but on lettuce, spinach, and other things, making the plants unattractive and unappealing to eat.

CORN AND TOMATO BORER: Bores into tomatoes and corn ears, making them unappetizing and causing gardeners to say the s word.

TOMATO HORNWORM: Eats tomato, pepper, eggplant, and potato foliage, and sometimes fruit. Hard to spot. Looks like a rolled up leaf. Finger size, light green, with creepy looking skin and a "horn" at back.

Usually only one per plant at a time. Voracious eaters. One critter can literally demolish an entire plant in a couple of days!

SQUASH BORER: The great terminator of squash, melon, pumpkin, and cucumber plants. Bores into the stem, near the base, and eats out the inside, leaving sawdust-like pulp.

◆ CUTWORM AND GRUBWORM: Beetle larvae. Under soil surface. Destroy roots, chew on root crops, and sometimes emerge from soil at night to nibble plants off at the stem.

◆ FLIES: Chew up foliage.

◆ LEAFMINERS: Teensy insect larvae that live *in* leaves, forming visible white "tracks."

◆ MAGGOTS: Fly larvae. Under soil surface. They eat roots and bore into onions and radishes.

◆ NEMATODES: Microscopic worms that live in soil or in roots. Most are harmful, causing stunted plant growth, wilted leaves, or poor fruit production (small, few). There are also beneficial types.

◆ PILL BUGS, ALSO KNOWN AS SOW BUGS OR ''ROLLY-POLLIES'': Attracted to dead plant debris, but also known to nibble on the living.

◆ SNAILS AND SLUGS: Similar, except a slug has no shell. Both hang out under moist cover, such as grass clipping mulch, during the day, coming out at night to feed on low-lying foliage and fruit.

◆ SPIDER MITES: Tiny members of spider family, hard to see. Produce very fine webs. Attack leaves, leaving tiny white spots. Severe infestations can substantially weaken plants.

As you can probably ascertain from the above descriptions, some critters are more harmful than others, i.e., the ones who eat the produce itself or kill entire plants. A few are considered "beneficials" — spiders, praying mantises, and ladybugs among them — eating other bugs and insects instead of your plants. However, as a practical matter, it's hard to distinguish between some good guys and some bad guys. And, unfortunately, insecticide doesn't discriminate.

I try to use a basically organic approach to kill pests. For those that are relatively large, easy to spot, easy to get at, and few in number, grab them and smush them. This will work, in most cases, for beetles, bugs, and caterpillars. To find them, inspect closely, and try to zero in on the most severe plant damage or fresh droppings.

When caterpillar infestations are too severe for bare knuckles, use BT, a bacteria that makes caterpillars too sick to eat, so that they starve to death. Inoculating your soil with a little BT powder at the start of the season should preclude most caterpillars from ever appearing. When the critters appear high up on plants later in the season, you can mist the foliage and sprinkle on granular BT "bait." It works like a charm.

Milky Spore is another beneficial bacteria, which kills grubworms and cutworms. It may take two or three seasons (and applications) to take full effect, but after that, you should never have to reapply.

For severe problems with squash borers, cutworms, grubworms, or maggots, you can inoculate your soil with nematodes. These are gross little microscopic parasitic worms that come in two types: a bad kind that afflicts plants, and a good kind that afflicts pests; make sure you buy the right kind (relax — you can only buy one kind). I haven't found them too effective, in my garden. Perhaps you'll have better results.

For aphids and flies, use insecticidal soap. It also minimizes damage from leafminers, if you catch them early enough. Mix your own solution in an old Windex bottle, and spray where needed. Don't waste it by prophylactic application on plants that aren't infested. And don't apply in extreme heat, as leaf damage will result. For aphids, especially treat new growth and the undersides of leaves. The stuff works surprisingly well, and it won't kill bees.

The best thing about most of the above products is not, in my opinion, that they're organic, but that they're easy. Other than the insecticidal soap, all are "fire-and-forget" weapons. And both BT and nematodes will often "winter over," at least in mild climates.

If none of the above works against a particular pest, try Rotenone, which is a fairly potent "natural" insecticide, derived from a tropical plant. Buy the liquid form, in the highest concentration available. Mix your own solution in an old spray bottle. Spray sparingly when and where needed. It kills good guys and bad guys, but at least it doesn't harm the environment.

The above products are available at many nurseries or can be ordered from:

> Gardens Alive
> 5100 Schenley Place
> Lawrenceburg, IN 47025

There are other organic pesticide methods, which, frankly, I find a little wacky. You can buy carnivorous "good guys," such as ladybugs, praying mantises, or wasps, to turn loose in your garden. Unfortunately, once they eat up the "bad guys," they move on or die. Some recommend trying to keep a small population of bad guys around for "dinner," but, hey, isn't that going a bit far? And you'll never catch me out at night with a flashlight, serving beer to slugs. Do keep in mind, however, that it's not necessary to eliminate every trace of pest damage from your garden; and even if you were intent on doing so, you would never succeed anyway.

As a last resort, I use regular old, bad-for-the-environment, chemical insecticides, such as Sevin, Diazinon, or Malathion. Don't, however, blast your entire garden weekly, with a spray apparatus that attaches to your hose. As with Rotenone and insecticidal soap, apply only when and where needed, mixing your solution in an old spritzer bottle. Unfortunately, the legally prescribed dosage on the label is usually about 25–50% weaker than what is really needed. I believe that if you're going to use the stuff, you shouldn't mess around. The worse thing you can do is use a solution just strong enough to kill 90% of the varmints, leaving the hardiest among them to reproduce. (However, *too* strong a solution — say, double or triple strength — would harm your plants.) Despite the label inferences (you are advised to throw out any solution you don't use at once), most solutions will keep for months.

The only effective way I've found to kill snails, slugs, and pill bugs (sow bugs) is snail and slug bait. It also is not particularly good for the environment, but it *is* safe enough for vegetable gardens. Moreover, you need not apply it directly *on* your plants. Since it's a "bait," it will draw the pests out.

Chemical insecticides *will* kill earthworms, if used very much over a very big area (the rain or sprinkler washes the insecticide off the foliage and down into the soil). Also keep in mind that both Rotenone and ordinary commercial insecticides kill honeybees. Not only do I *like* bees, we *need* them for pollination. So spray late in the day, after bees have gone home for the night, and avoid getting it on (and, especially, *in*) blossoms.

Be sure to label all the spray bottles you fill with various concoctions, especially if you also mix up different solutions for ornamentals (I keep *ornamental* insect spray and also fungicide mixtures on hand). If you go for your gun in haste and accidentally spray ornamental insecticide on your spinach, you won't be able to eat it and may contaminate your vegetable soil. If your family can't use Windex fast enough to provide all these bottles, you can buy ready-mixed insecticides in spray bottles at the nursery. They're a little expensive, but when the bottles are used up, you can refill them with your own mixes, corresponding to the labels already on the bottles. It's much cheaper to mix your own, and just as effective.

Most of the *diseases* that afflict vegetable gardens are various forms of wilt and blight, caused by bacteria or fungus. Wilt is partial to tomatoes and vining plants, starting out with isolated branches, then often eventually causing entire plants to wilt and die. Blight, also partial to tomatoes, causes spots on the leaves; it too can eventually weaken and kill plants. The bacterial forms of both are sometimes transmitted by beetles. If you find that your plants are coming down with either wilt or blight, remove the infected branches and destroy them. But it may be too late.

Other diseases afflicting the vegetable patch include: downy mildew, a fungus that covers leaves and fruit with furry growth; "mosaic," a viral disease, often transmitted by aphids, that causes distorted, stunted leaves and fruit — especially in squash; and corn smut, which is a fungal disease infecting corn, described in the section on sweet corn.

When it comes to *diseases*, as opposed to *pests*, there are few products you can apply that are safe enough for your family's vegetable garden. *Prevention* is the thing. Practice crop rotation. Plant disease-resistant varieties, particularly if you've been bothered by a specific problem in the past. Don't leave decaying plant debris (dead squash leaves, pruned tomato branches, etc.) lying around on the surface of your beds. Don't water at night, as things stay too wet, which encourages fungus; water in the morning (except during seed germination, when late afternoon is best). Most of all, if a plant contracts a disease, GET RID OF IT. Carefully remove it, roots and all if possible, seal it in a plastic bag, and put it in the garbage — not the compost pile!

ALTERNATIVES

CONTAINER GARDENING

There are several possible reasons to grow vegetables in pots rather than raised beds. You may live in an apartment or condo, with a sunny balcony but no yard. You may rent your house, from a grumpy landlord who doesn't like gardens or thinks dirt looks strange in boxes. You may want to extend the growing season for a particular crop — containers offer the flexibility to move plants indoors on cool nights or into the shade on hot days. You may have run out of room in your raised beds but still have one or two other things you really want to grow. Or you might just like the looks. Everyone grows ivy and philodendrons in pots. Why not vegetables? Many vegetable plants are quite attractive.

If you're growing "containerized" veggies for any reason other than the last one, those black plastic pots that shrubs and trees come in from the nursery are ideal. Or consider using containers never intended for growing plants, that would otherwise be thrown out with the trash. Just don't forget to cut some holes in the bottoms for drainage.

Throwaway plastic containers can provide a miniature raised, intensive-bed garden, in locations where aesthetics are not important.

Most vegetables can be grown in containers. Some do better at it than others. In principle, there's no difference between a raised bed and a large pot. Both use an artificial structure to hold dirt up off the ground. However, as a practical matter, no one would build a raised bed just 12 or 18 inches in diameter.

Pots do confine root growth more than raised beds. If you try to grow too big a plant in too small a pot, the restricted root growth will in turn restrict top growth and fruit size. It will also make the soil dry out faster, as the struggling plant sucks up every bit of moisture just to stay alive.

Actually, even a plant in an "appropriate"-sized container will never attain the size of one grown in a larger patch of earth. I'm not really sure why. I presume extra-generous space means extra-ambitious root growth, even if it's in competition with other plants in your garden. And, of course, a raised bed has dirt below, even if it's not very good dirt. When roots in a pot reach the bottom, that's it.

And even appropriate-sized plants in appropriate-sized pots need to be watered more frequently than raised beds. The warm air and sun surrounding both a raised bed and a pot cause the soil to warm up, evaporating moisture faster than "in-ground" dirt. But a pot has a higher ratio of outside surface to inside dirt. So the soil tends to be warmer, especially if the pot is black. Dark colors, of course, absorb heat more than lighter colors. That can be an advantage in cool climates, or a disadvantage in hot ones.

Fertilize container vegetables with the same type fertilizers you would use in a garden. But use less of it, and do it a little more often. For example, use 1/4 cup of 5–10–10 for a tomato or pepper in a 12-inch pot, instead of the half cup you would use in the garden.

What to grow in pots? Obviously not watermelons or pumpkins. Too confining. Or corn — you could never grow a big enough stand to get good pollination. But just about all small to mid-sized plants are fair game. Vegetables that readily lend themselves to container culture include tomatoes, peppers, eggplant, lettuce, spinach, green onions, radishes, potatoes, and sweet potatoes.

Herbs are especially well adapted to container growing. The most commonly grown ones are tarragon, sage, mint, basil, chives, savory, rosemary, thyme, and parsley. Basil, parsley, and one type of savory ("summer" savory) are annuals. All of the others mentioned are perennials.

For tomatoes, your best bet is to grow a small, determinate variety, such as Patio, Pixie, or Bitsy. All will produce fruit about two inches in diameter, i.e., bigger than cherry tomatoes but less than hamburger size. These plants will do fine in pots 12–15 inches in diameter and of similar depth. If you scale your pot down much smaller, best stick with "basket" cherry tomato varieties, like Tiny Tim. Obviously, bigger tomato varieties need bigger pots,

Patio tomato in 12-inch pot

but it's difficult to get a truly large-fruited variety such as Better Boy to do well, even in an oversized pot.

All peppers will do well in 12–15-inch containers, but don't expect large-fruited bell peppers to produce the same size fruit that they would in a garden. Small-fruited peppers, such as sweet bananas, sweet or hot cherries, jalapeños, and cayennes, are much better adapted to container growing.

144

Chili pepper in wooden planter

Small-fruited eggplants also do better than large-fruited ones; they require the same size containers as tomatoes and peppers.

Lettuce, spinach, radishes, and green onions do not require very deep containers. Six inches will do it, although it's hard to find a plant pot that shallow that is wide enough to grow as many of these guys as you would want — that's where oddball, throwaway containers come in handy.

Potatoes and sweet potatoes do best in containers somewhat larger — say, 18 inches wide and the same in depth (you'll be surprised how many full-size potatoes a large container will provide!). The drawback is that pots this big are expensive ... and not very portable, once they are filled with dirt.

Among herbs, parsley and savory can be grown in smaller flower pots, around 8–10 inches in diameter. The other herbs mentioned above should be planted in somewhat larger containers.

Sweet potato vines make attractive patio plants . . .

There are several vegetables that *can* be grown in containers, but with varied success. One such animal is squash. If you're going to try it, use a container at least 18 inches wide and deep, and stick to the smaller, "limited space" varieties. Bush beans grow well in containers, but it's difficult to grow enough of them to be worthwhile. Ditto for carrots and full-size onions, which have the additional problem of not always forming the most desirable shape and size roots when grown in containers.

GARDEN IN A CAN

Here's a trick that even people with large gardens, who need not otherwise grow container veggies, will want to try. Buy a plastic outdoor garbage can on sale for a few dollars. Cut some one-inch holes in the bottom. Then fill it

. . . and can produce an amazing number
of tubers.

with good soil. It will cost only a fraction of what you would pay for a large pot *designed* to grow plants. It may only be a little bigger in diameter, but it will probably be twice the depth, and it will hold several times the *volume* of dirt. In a "garbage can garden," you *can* grow a full-size squash or icebox melon plant! But the biggest advantage for those of us who *have* gardens is the *depth* of good soil a garbage can provides. With the luxury of excellent soil that goes down two or three feet deep, you can grow giant parsnips or Daikon radishes that will amaze your neighbors.

COLD-CLIMATE GARDENING

It seems that gardening books are always written for folks in Maryland or Ohio, who have fairly lengthy growing seasons, with cool nights and moderately warm days. You can grow almost anything in such a climate, at one time of year or another. But what if you are not so blessed? The first step is to "change the things over which you have some control."

If you're gardening in an unusually cold climate, you've already taken the first step toward stacking the deck in your favor — or at least giving yourself a fighting chance: raised beds. They increase the internal heat of your soil substantially. Painting the wooden frames flat black will encourage even more heat, since black absorbs, rather than reflects, heat.

Increase the heat of your raised bed still further by using a layer of black plastic on the soil surface, especially in spring and fall, leaving "holes" where the plants are. Also punch numerous tiny pinprick holes, with an icepick or scissors, to allow water to soak into the entire bed. You won't have to water too often, as the "plastic mulch" reduces evaporation from the soil. The plastic can be stapled to the wooden bed frames. If you like, rather than paint your boxes black, you can drape the black plastic all the way to the bottoms of the frames.

Black plastic can also hasten seed germination. For example, you can plant turnip, carrot, or radish seed, then lay black plastic over the entire seedbed, weighting it down with a few rocks or bricks. Just be sure to peek under occasionally. The plastic must be removed, of course, when the plants start sprouting.

One way to stretch the growing season is to start everything from transplants that can reasonably be started from transplants. In addition to the obvious ones — tomatoes, peppers, eggplant, greens, and coles — give your squash, melons, and cucumbers a head start as well (assuming your climate is warm enough to accommodate these plants at all). Tomatoes and peppers can be given an *extra* head start by repotting to larger pots, sinking them deeper into the soil each time, leaving only a small amount of foliage above the soil line. And do start your onions from plants rather than sets. When raising onions from transplants, crop the tops by about half when they are planted; this will get them off to a more vigorous start.

Another trick is to enclose individual tomato, pepper, eggplant, and squash plants in cages (even if you don't intend to leave the cages indefinitely), with clear plastic wrapped around the cages. The plastic acts as a greenhouse: ultraviolet light can get in, warming things up, but infrared radiation (essentially, heat) can't get out. Make sure each cage has an opening on top, adequate for ventilation, especially when days are warm. A large plastic soda bottle, with the top removed and bottom cut off, makes a handy mini-greenhouse for small plants; punch some holes down low to create an updraft.

As the sun begins to set, place an insulated cover over each plant for the night. A bag made out of heavy cloth or an old quilt is good. Even better is a throwaway styrofoam ice chest (weight it down with a brick, so it won't blow away), as long as the cage is small enough to fit inside. These techniques will work for several weeks in the spring and fall, but you'll not want to pursue them all summer. Not only is it too much trouble (for me anyway), but "plastic wrap" interferes with honeybee pollination.

And none of the above is to imply that given enough plastic — clear or black — you can successfully grow warm weather plants in an area where summer temperatures rarely exceed 70 or 75. Nor will plastic enable warm weather plants to survive hard frosts ... or thrive in mild frosts. Plastic

Coke bottle greenhouse for new tomato transplant. Bed has been
draped in perforated black plastic.

coverings *can* enable warm weather plants to *survive* mild frosts, but, actually,
the main benefit of both clear plastic coverings and nighttime protection is
that they raise the average temperature your plants enjoy by 10 degrees or so.
If the only danger is nighttime frost, and daytime temperatures are adequate,
you may want to forgo the plastic wrap and just apply nighttime protection.

The most important variable over which you "have control" is plant variety. Cool-climate gardeners will want fast-maturing varieties, tolerant to
cool weather, especially when it comes to tomatoes, peppers, and green
beans. Varieties accustomed to warm weather are susceptible to disease when
grown under cool — and especially *cool, damp* — conditions. Some corn
varieties mature in 60–75 days, compared to about 90 for most in "Middle
America." The faster maturing corn tends to grow smaller plants and smaller
ears, which, frankly, are not quite as good as most of the longer-maturing
varieties…but you do what you can do.

So much for controlling the negatives. As Bing would have said, you should also accentuate the positives. Some vegetables were *created* for cool climates. Peas, broccoli, cauliflower, spinach, lettuce, carrots, potatoes, radishes, beets, and turnips all perform wonderfully with daytime temperatures in the 60's and 70's, even if nighttime temps are in the 30's or 40's. Rutabagas will *only* grow in areas with long, cool summers. Gardeners grow humongous cabbages in Alaska and mammoth radishes in northern Japan, made possible only because of the long, cool summers. Crops that are considered short-lived spring or fall vegetables in most parts of America will often grow all summer in exceptionally cool climates. For color and variety, try some ornamental cabbage.

Don't waste your time and soil trying to grow things not adapted to your climate. If daytime temperatures never exceed the 70's in your area, you'll

A good cool-climate selection: Brussels sprouts, broccoli, ornamental cabbage, recently transplanted onions (tops cut back), green and red leaf lettuce, spinach. . .and one small dog.

Giant cabbage grown in Anchorage, Alaska

Japanese radishes fit for Godzilla

never win trying to grow corn, cucumbers, melons, peppers, or tomatoes. I tried twice to grow tomatoes in Germany; one year I succeeded…in harvesting two red, vine-ripened, golfball-size-fruits, from a withered plant, a few days before the first fall frost rolled in. Even in regions with daytime summer temperatures regularly in the low 80's, you're fighting a hopeless battle with a truly hot-weather tropical like okra — by the time the plants are big enough to produce pods, cool weather will already be setting in for the fall and the pods will start turning woody. The final step, then, is to "accept the things you can't control."

HOT-CLIMATE GARDENING

When we moved to south Texas, after three years in chilly central Europe, my mouth watered at the thought of an eight-month vegetable growing season. Little did I know that almost nothing would grow in San Antonio during the 100 degree days from May 15 to October 1! When I realized our yard consisted of two inches of topsoil, atop almost solid rock and caliche, I constructed some raised beds and ordered a truckload of a landscaper's "special garden mix" (which turned out to be mostly sand). After one summer of runty corn and tomato blossoms that wouldn't set fruit, I sat back and analyzed the situation.

One conclusion was that the deep South, far from having one long growing season, really has two short ones — spring and fall. Very short ones, at that. True, spring comes early. But it doesn't last long. In San Antonio, frost is not uncommon in late March, so you're taking a chance to put your tomatoes out before April Fool's. Yet, by May 15, 100-degree weather often sets in. Tomato vines start to wither; blossoms stop setting fruit. The 100-degree heat doesn't end in the Alamo city until October 1, when folks up north are stocking up on firewood, yet Jack Frost frequently arrives as early as mid-November in south Texas. In some respects, then, gardening in areas that have extremely hot summers (but frequent frost in winter), is like gardening in northern New England or Minnesota. You have to squeeze as much growing as you can into the short gardening seasons.

That means, for instance, using fast maturing varieties for crops that don't do well in extreme heat, even if that risks appearing foolish to Burpee for ordering tomatoes specially bred for Vermont when you live in Phoenix. It means taking a chance and planting some things early in the spring, covering and protecting them as best you can on cold nights, all the while standing by to replant if need be. It means planting your fall Brussels sprouts in the blistering August sun, then trying to keep them alive until the weather tempers.

On the plus side, if you live in area with extremely hot summers, chances are you can grow some things all winter, even if you have frost. Lettuce, cole crops, turnips, radishes, and parsnips will tolerate mild frosts. Spinach, onions, and Romaine lettuce will all survive severe frosts.

But what about summer? Do you let the raised beds you worked so hard on sit fallow for three to five months, during which time similar beds in most of the country are at their peak productivity? Not on your life. Your next task is to seek out vegetables that will survive extreme heat. Squash is one such plant. It may not be as gorgeous in July as its cousin in North Carolina. The leaves may droop during the afternoon. And perhaps not every blossom will open properly — thus, not every fruit will set or develop properly. It *can* be done, however.

But wait. There's more. There are a number of vegetables that will not only *survive* extreme heat but will actually thrive in it. Melons, okra, peppers, sweet potatoes, and Swiss chard all fall into this category, as do portulaca and gazanias if you're looking for some color. It never ceases to amaze me in Texas. When it is 103 in our back yard, my okra is eight feet tall, with woody trunks four inches in diameter, and producing so prolifically that we can't

Winter lettuce will survive mild frosts,
while spinach will endure through even
hard frosts.

keep up with it (in fact, we can't even *reach* the pods on top). My sweet potatoes grow to enormous proportions, blessed with a six-month growing
season. And long after my spring tomato plants look like lepers, my pepper
bushes are four feet tall and two feet wide, loaded with fruit and fresh
blossoms that never fail to set.

A good hot-climate selection: okra,
peppers, and portulaca.

Do pay attention to those "recommended varieties" advocated for your area by your state agriculture department. They're not always the ones Burpee puts the bullseyes on. For example, super-sweet corn tends not to pollinate well in extreme heat, but Merit (a "normal" sweet corn) does great. Beefsteak tomatoes tend to scald, crack, and ripen unevenly in very hot climates, while smaller-fruited varieties such as Celebrity do much better.

Tomatoes that are even smaller-fruited, like Roma, not only ripen well in fairly intense heat, but the blossoms set better.

Most tomato varieties will not set fruit if you have many days with temperatures much above 90. The blossoms simply fall off. Spraying with "blossom set" helps, but it's a lot of trouble, and it sometimes makes for misshapen fruit. Anyway, it somehow seems like cheating to me. Applying extra phosphorous at transplanting time is almost as effective.

One way I've found to grow tomatoes successfully in extreme heat is to cage them and then tie a wooden lath lattice across the top. At first I was surprised that it worked, since the lattice filters out two thirds of the light, which I thought would be too much sun loss for healthy photosynthesis. It's true that in the morning, when the sun is low, and the temperatures cooler, my plants received some beneficial direct light. However, the sun is just as low in the afternoon, when it's hot as Hell, and I was afraid that that might do my plants in. Whatever…it works. Eventually, the plants will grow up through the lattice, which provides extra support. Although the blossom drop above the lattice is significant, a surprising number of fruit will set, especially if you're growing one of the more heat-tolerant varieties. Possibly the shade on the vines beneath the lattice has a beneficial effect on the entire plant.

Whether spring, summer, or fall crops, you should optimize every factor you can control, to reduce the effects of the heat. Provide your soil extra humus, to retain moisture better. Use a one- or two-inch layer of mulch on top of the soil. Dried grass clippings are good; their fine texture increases moisture retention, compared to other mulches, while their light color reflects heat better. Try to provide some shade. You can build wooden frames over your beds and cover them with plastic mesh to provide filtered shade. In Texas I tried planting heat-sensitive plants directly north of my okra, to give them some shade. It didn't work. There was *too much* shade. However, if you can time it right, try siting heat-sensitive plants to the north of your spring

Caged tomato plants topped with a lath lattice for filtered shade

Plants will eventually grow up through the lattice.

corn; after the corn is harvested, leave the stalks to wither and provide filtered shade.

Ideally, you would like a way to cool your beds *without* reducing the sun. But, short of air conditioning, dream on.

Chapter

6

THE TEN MOST COMMON MISTAKES IN VEGETABLE GARDENING

My first vegetable garden was pretty disappointing. I thought all I had to do was stick some seeds in the ground, water them, then stand back. Most things sprouted. Some plants grew, but weren't really too healthy looking. A few even produced fruit. I learned from my mistakes and started seeking advice from more experienced gardeners. My second garden was much better — perhaps even as good as the *average* American vegetable plot. My third attempt was actually quite successful. And my garden was the envy of the neighborhood the following year, when I suddenly realized that I had become the one folks *turned* to for advice.

Probably the most common question vegetable gardeners ask each other is, "What am I doing wrong?" In response to that, based on both my own experience and observing other gardeners at work, I offer, in order of significance, the most common mistakes in vegetable gardening:

1. NEGLECT. I have no proof, but I feel confident this is the number 1 reason vegetable gardens fail. In the springtime, all over America, gardeners return home from nurseries with car trunks full of peat moss, bark mulch, dried sheep manure, and tomato fertilizer spikes. There is a frenzy of gardening activity in the back yard all weekend. By mid summer, the garden is full of weeds, plants are brown from lack of water, and leathery fruit rots on the vine. By *late* summer, the family even leaves on vacation without worrying about the garden being untended. "What the heck," they say, "it's not doing much anyway." Gardens do require a certain amount of work (though not much, if you set them up right). And there's no such thing as "benign neglect." At the very least, a successful garden must be *looked at* daily. Otherwise, you'll never know when pepper branches require support, when a hornworm starts eating your tomato plant (he can finish the task in two days), or when your corn has fallen over from wind and rain.

2. HARD-PACKED SOIL. For those who *are* willing to fool around with their gardens a little every day, and stick with it, the most common reason for failure is probably inadequately prepared soil. Roots do not grow well in dense soil. Most back yards consist of either sandy soil, which dries easily into a concrete-like substance, or black topsoil, which is sticky and gummy when wet and forms big, hard clods when dry. Even if you dig the soil and bust the clods, given rain or sprinkling and a month's time, such dirt eventually settles back into its original state. Repeated walking on the soil only hastens and worsens the inevitable. The first type of dirt above needs to be supplemented with topsoil, the second type with sand. And they both cry out for humus. Better yet are raised beds, where *you* control the soil mix and the garden never gets trampled.

3. POOR DRAINAGE. Everyone knows plants need water, but it's hard to convince new gardeners that plants also need drainage. Roots require air, as well as moisture. The usual cause of poor drainage is rock and clay a few inches beneath the topsoil. The most obvious solution is to dig down a foot, remove the offending substances, cart them away, and refill the newly created excavation with good soil. In most cases, however, this is so much work as to be impractical. And it doesn't always do the trick, for rock and clay surrounding and underlying the garden can turn your new improved soil into a "cup" that winds up collecting water despite its own admirable qualities. Of course, you can always just try to find another area for your garden. But raised beds are the easiest and most effective solution.

4. LACK OF "GOOD SOIL" DEPTH. Your garden consists of improved soil, which gets dug and spaded and supplemented with humus, on top of—unless you're very lucky—poorer subsoil. Often, the "good soil" isn't deep enough for particular crops. Many "traditional" gardeners compound the problem by continual shoveling at the same depth; the tip of the shovel can compact the soil just below into a virtually impenetrable hardpan. As with problems 2 and 3, raised beds facilitate solving this one, because they add good soil to whatever you have underneath.

5. RUSHING THINGS. After licking their lips over graph paper and seed catalogs all winter, gardeners rush out and buy trays full of tomato and pepper plants as soon as the plants appear in the nursery. The seedlings are driven home, where they are babied for one week—repotted, watered, brought in at night. As soon as three consecutive days of nice spring weather occur, gardeners decide to get a jump on things and plant early. A week later, "Indian winter" hits, and everyone's out in the dark trying to cover their babies up for a cold night. Wait *at least* until the recommended earliest planting date for your area. An extra week or two is better. Even if you're lucky and don't get frost, warm weather plants don't grow while days are still cool and nights cold; in fact, quite the opposite — they suffer a setback.

6. INSUFFICIENT LIGHT FOR HOME-STARTED SEEDLINGS. For those who start their own tomato, pepper, eggplant, lettuce, and cole plants indoors, it's essential to have a grow light. This is the main reason most gardeners try starting their own plants just once, then give up and return to the nursery the next year. Keep the light one to two inches from the tops of the plants, for 14 hours a day, using a timer.

7. INSUFFICIENT HARDENING. This is the other reason most "self-starters" give up after their first attempt. Seedlings started indoors need about two weeks of acclimatizing before going into the garden. Find a spot outdoors that gets sun for only half a day — morning, if possible — or 50% filtered sun throughout the day, and where about two thirds of the wind is blocked. Bring the plants in when temperatures drop below 50.

8. SHALLOW WATERING. Frequent, shallow watering promotes root growth near the top of the soil, with little down deep. This hurts in two ways: not enough total root growth, and the danger of plants dying if they must go without water for a few days, since the upper soil layer dries out first. For healthy plants, it's essential to water deep, and far better to do it less often.

9. TOO MUCH NITROGEN. Use about one styrofoam coffee cup of 5–10–10 fertilizer (5% nitrogen, 10% phosphorous, 10% potassium) for 4–8 square feet of garden surface, for most vegetables — including tomatoes, peppers, eggplant, carrots, potatoes, turnips, radishes, and squash. Use the same amount of 15–10–10 for corn, lettuce, spinach, cabbage family members, and other leafy greens. BUT use the latter on the former and you'll get all leaves with no fruit.

10. WRONG SEED VARIETY FOR REGION. This happens most often in extreme climates, such as northern New England or southern Arizona. If you don't live in a "gardening mainstream" state, make sure you choose varieties tested and proven for your area. Those seeds with the asterisks in the seed

catalogs, signifying the best all-around selections for most U.S. gardeners, are not necessarily the ones you want.

So there you have it. Every gardener knows the above factors are important, but sometimes we niggle and try to "get by." New gardeners especially are prone to such mistakes. But believe it. All 10 matter. They say that everything worth doing is worth doing right. And the point is, it's not hard to do everything right if you do it from the start.

RULES OF MODERN VEGETABLE GARDENING

1. Use raised beds. 4 feet wide, 4–10 feet long, framed with lumber. Make sure your "good soil" is at least 12 inches deep, counting your raised bed, plus whatever you improve below.

2. Plant intensively. No rows. No paths.

3. Keep your garden small and manageable. Just big enough to accomplish your goals. It's more rewarding to do a little bit well than a lot poorly.

4. The ideal soil, in general, is approximately one part sand, two parts top-soil, and one part organic matter. Regularly add humus, and use a variety, to insure that necessary trace minerals are supplied.

5. Fertilize with 5–10–10 or 15–10–10 (depending on the type of vegetable), at a rate of 1/8–1/4 cup per square foot.

6. Rotate your crops.

7. Try organic methods of insecticide first, but use common sense. Spray chemical insecticides if necessary, on a limited basis, from a "spritzer" bottle; mix your own, to save money.

8. Order seed from mail order companies. The selection is better.

9. Start your own transplants. It's the only way to get some varieties.

10. Garden for fresh taste — and fun. Only can, freeze, and pickle if that's fun for you. Produce is cheap in America. It's just not very tasty most of the time.

INDEX